ERIN PETTENGILL

TERMITES ATE MY COUCH

TRUE STORIES OF A MISSIONARY NURSE

Advantage
BOOKS

Termites Ate My Couch by Erin T. Pettengill, RN, BSN, MPH
Copyright © 2017 by Erin T. Pettengill
All Rights Reserved.
ISBN: 978-1-59755-435-0

Published by: ADVANTAGE BOOKS™
Longwood, Florida, USA
www.advbookstore.com

Scripture quotations are from The ESV® Bible (The Holy Bible, English Standard Version®), copyright © 2001 by Crossway, a publishing ministry of Good News Publishers. Used by permission. All rights reserved.

Library of Congress Catalog Number: 2017939681

First Printing: June 2017
17 18 19 20 21 22 23   10 9 8 7 6 5 4 3 2 1
Printed in the United States of America

Dedication

This book is dedicated to my husband, Mike, who is my best friend, my ally, my support, my partner in life, the half to my whole and who encouraged me to put my words to paper.

Also, to my sweet daughter, Madison, who helped make me into the person I am today.

To my brother, Tom, who has helped me get through the grief of the passing of our parents, who is creative and funny, and who loves me dearly.

My mother and father who guided me along in this crazy thing we call life, but who both passed away before they knew this book was even in the making – but I know they would have been proud to see this a reality.

Finally, without whom this book could never have made it to its final presentation, my editor, Rebecca Blunk – she helped turn my thoughts into the stories that you are about to read.

Thank you to all.

"What then shall we say to these things? If God is for us, who can be against us? He who did not spare his own Son but gave him up for us all, how will he not also with him graciously give us all things? Who shall bring any charge against God's elect? It is God who justifies. Who is to condemn? Christ Jesus is the one who died—more than that, who was raised—who is at the right hand of God, who indeed is interceding for us. Who shall separate us from the love of Christ? Shall tribulation, or distress, or persecution, or famine, or nakedness, or danger, or sword? As it is written, 'For your sake we are being killed all the day long; we are regarded as sheep to be slaughtered.' No, in all these things we are more than conquerors through him who loved us. For I am sure that neither death nor life, nor angels nor rulers, nor things present nor things to come, nor powers, nor height nor depth, nor anything else in all creation, will be able to separate us from the love of God in Christ Jesus our Lord." - Romans 8:31–39

Foreword

What you are about to read is more than a collection of stories. It is about a journey. A journey of a woman, a nurse, a soldier, a daughter, a mother, a sister, a wife, a missionary, a citizen of the world finding her path while avoiding obstructions of physical and mental blocks to achieve more in her lifetime than most have even dared dream about. This journey wasn't easy.

This is more than just a collection of short stories with a clear-cut setup, a few trials for the protagonist to overcome and then some easy happy ending all wrapped up in a nice, neat bow. This story is full of hardship, triumph over tragedy, conflict of body and soul, and is more a journey of spirit rather than physical miles.

It's important to note that during her spiritual journey she has indeed traveled many thousands of miles, visiting and living in countries all over the world—from her home in California to her time in the military stationed in Germany; from the adopted home of her missionary life in Honduras to her current home, the impoverished nation of Equatorial Guinea in Africa.

I, being her brother, have had a unique perspective on my sister's travels. While I have made very different decisions, taking the left path while she went right, I can say without reservation that Erin is one of the finest people I have ever met.

We disagree politically, philosophically, ideologically, and on matters of faith we couldn't be further apart. While she has found answers in her spiritual studies, I have found a more worldly view on life better serves my views on society and the human condition.

I often ask myself how two children brought up in the same environment can be so opposite, but I have come to realize that Erin's faith is what fuels her: it's what drives her and helps her to accomplish amazing things.

I consider my atheism constantly renewed by experience and intellectual consideration. However, if there is one person who makes me question the existence of a divine presence it is my sister.

Our mother, to supplement her income and help pay her college tuition, used to do Tarot card readings. In this symbolic language of the Tarot, the sword represents thought. Actually it's much deeper than that; it is the entire realm of the conscious mind. An untrained mind is figuratively, and literally, translated through this imagery as a dull and ineffectual sword which will serve the bearer poorly. A sharp and focused sword is needed for growth of spirit and truth.

For the Christian, the sword means even more. The sword in Christianity characterizes righteousness, justice and protection. The sword is a weapon of faith.

However, it is important to understand that not all swords are created equal. A sword is forged through destruction. Through trial. through fire and hard work. Sure, you can pick up a stick and swing it wildly trying to defend yourself, but against a real sword forged through skill and patience, that stick will fail you and you will find yourself literally in a world of hurt.

Within these stories we see the anvil on which Erin herself has been forged, how she has been shaped and wrought into the person she is today—a woman of truth, of spirit, of faith and superior character. She is a brilliant sword and a formidable weapon in the hand of her Maker.

Table of Contents

Chapter 1

The Taxi Ride

In the taxi I rode... around the city... and around and around. Through the cracked windshield I could see women shopping with their infants strapped to their backs, venders selling their wares, and people hocking homemade bread and fresh-grown lettuce. I was amazed as the driver wove his way through the chaos of the disorganized assemblage of vegetable stands and people in the center of the town of Bata.

Finally the taxi driver pulled up in front of a building. Instead of getting out, I sat anxiously on the ripped seat. I did not recognize where we were, and the driver was asking me where to go. He spoke in Spanish with an accent that was heavily mixed with Castilian and Fang – the local tribal language. Feeling mild panic, I looked at him in complete bewilderment. I told him I had no clue. I had only been in country for one week, and I was relying upon him to get me where I needed to go.

With a heavy sigh, he turned back to the road in front of him, turned up his Reggaeton music, and on we went. During our drive through town, three additional passengers got in the taxi and were taken to their destination. Then two more passengers got in and were taken to their destination. And on we went. I pulled out my phone and had my husband's phone number up, ready to hit "dial" in case things went bad. I was in Africa after all...things do go "bad" here.

About forty minutes into my ride, the driver finally pulled up in front of a building I DID recognize. He turned to me and asked me if this was where I wanted to go. With a sigh, an inward rush of relief, and a "Si, y que Dios le Bendiga," (YES! And may God bless you), I got out.

Week one…in a new country…once again…

****

My adventure began more than eleven years earlier on the day my husband returned home from a short-term mission trip to Belize. It was there he was prompted by God to pursue missions on a full-time basis, and he had to figure out how to break the news to me.

We went out to a nice dinner, he ordered a bottle of wine, and then he started wringing his hands. *Hmmm*, I thought, *We are already married – HAPPILY so. HE can't be pregnant ... so what gives?*

"Out with it!" I said.

In a rush, so he couldn't think too much about it or take it back, he said, "I think we need to do this missions thing full-time." And he sat back, waiting for the shoe to drop – on his head, I think.

Unbeknownst to me he had already bargained with God, telling Him, "Fine. I will be obedient, but Erin won't want to go." I was a nurse manager on a general pediatric hematology/oncology floor. I had worked there for twelve years and absolutely LOVED my job. Mike thought there was no chance was I going to put all that aside to basically go work for free in a third world country with little to no resources. No WAY! Since there was no chance I would agree to go, he wouldn't have to do it after all. I was his "easy out."

"Okay!" I responded.

The most comical look came across his face. There I was— blowing his chance to get out of this whole mission thing. He confessed to me later that he was going into this kicking and screaming. But there I was, telling God, "Yes! Yes, I will go for you! For YOU, because I wouldn't go for me.

Chapter 2

So... am I Donatello, Raphael, Michelangelo or Leonardo?

"But the Lord is faithful. He will establish you and guard you against the evil one." - 2 Thessalonians 3:3

I am sure that many a missionary has great stories to tell about their "beginnings." There are stories of overcoming obstacles, of landing on riverbanks in small yellow airplanes, bringing freedom through Christ in their every act. There are those who braved China and were faithful to receive all things through prayer. Then there are others like me who have such humble beginnings.

I didn't come upon my faith in a very traditional manner. I grew up in an amazing household. My mother and my father were incredible examples of what a loving marital relationship should be like. But neither of them were believers. As a matter of fact, my mother was a Wicca witch. She believed in the spiritual world, in the balance of nature, in giving and receiving equally. The biggest holiday we celebrated at our house was Halloween. We would spend months creating props and decorations for the house, turning it into the best haunted house in the neighborhood. For a time, we had a palm-reading service in our household, and my mother read tarot cards. My mother divined spirits and absorbed energy from the departed. My father constructed a pyramid in our living room for my mother. To a wicca, a pyramid harnesses energy, and she wanted her children protected. But, in order to watch television, my brother and I had to sit under the pyramid because it took up the ENTIRE living room.

I don't tell any of this information to belittle my mother's beliefs. She was a fierce believer in the spiritual world. She loved the teachings of Buddha, Jesus and Mohammed and was a woman of moral values and high standards. She was also very welcoming of all things spiritual. The local Young Life meeting was often held in our living room. Whenever there was need for a place to hold the fifty to seventy-five Young Life kids, I only needed to ask and permission was given. My parents had so much faith in us that they would leave the house to the Young Life group while it was going on and go out to eat. Most kids called them "Mom and Dad Brumm." It was through Young Life that God captured me and turned my heart to Him at the age of fifteen.

****

That initial dinner conversation with my husband led to a year and a half of evaluation sessions, interviews, and training by our mission sending agency as they prepared us to head to the mission field. We learned how to live cross-culturally, learn a language, raise support, promote ourselves in churches, and live as nomads as we travelled across the country and back several times.

Now Mike, our daughter Madison and I were headed to New York for a final month of training from our mission agency. There we would learn about cross-cultural ministry, language-acquisition, and a host of other things to prepare us to go full-time on the mission field. We flew into New York's JFK airport on a red-eye flight, totally sleep-deprived, and the apartment we were staying in was on the other side of Manhattan.

If you know my husband at all, you know that he is the penny pincher of all penny pinchers. Not only had we taken a red-eye flight to get to New York (it was cheaper after all), but my sweet husband had decided, against the advice of our mission agency, that we were going to take the public transportation system to get to our apartment instead of a taxi. We had diligently studied the metro maps and planned out our path. He was convinced that it was going to be "super easy" to get from JFK to Washington Heights.

It was a Sunday…in the middle of construction. But we didn't know any of that. Sunday and construction. The first meant that a large majority of subway trains didn't run that day – certainly no "express" trains. So the ones we had so carefully plotted out didn't run where we needed to go. We kept getting on and getting off of trains until we really didn't know where we were. After a LOT of consultation with metro maps, we finally spied the train we needed, and on we got. And then it stopped...two stations later. "Construction," the conductor announced on the intercom, "Everyone off. You will need to take the bus from here to your final destination." Seriously? Okay… deep breath… off we got…

We got out, looked up, and found that we were three stories underground, and there was no working elevator to get us to street level. I looked at the bags we had brought with us. We were going to be here for a month, after all, and there were three of us. So, we had each brought two 50-pound bags – the limit with the airlines. But I looked at my sweet nine-year-old daughter and knew there was NO chance she would ever be able to carry a fifty-pound bag up three flights of stairs. And let me clarify, being "cheap" also meant we didn't have suitcases – we were using our U.S. Army duffel bags. What does that mean? No rolling bags: no nice, easy means to transport them –nothing but a single hand strap and two straps to carry it like a backpack.

I looked at Mike, he looked at me, and we came up with a plan. He would carry a fifty-pound bag on his back, and another fifty-pound bag in each of his hands; and I would have to do the same. There simply was no other way. I like to think that I'm in fairly good shape, but not since U.S. Army Jump School had I challenged my body to carry an extra 150 pounds, and certainly not up three full flights of stairs.

Mike was already jamming up the stairs. So, with my child in front of me, up the stairs I climbed. And climbed…and climbed…until I was just getting ready to round the last and final set of stairs, when the most unfortunate thing happened. I was SO tired, I didn't lift my foot high enough. When I went to take the last step, my foot caught on the lip of the stair and over I fell. I fell on top of the duffel bag that was on my back, and both my hands were caught on the straps of the bags I had in each hand. There I went—backwards—head first—down an entire flight of stairs, dragging all of the bags with me.

I landed at the bottom, and I could feel my eyes open wide. I was shocked, but I was also assessing. Could I move my arms and feet? Did I know who I was? Was I intact? I was able to pull my hands out from under the two bags at my side and looked at all the skin that had torn from the backs of my hands. But I couldn't move—I was still strapped to the duffel bag that was on my back.

Poor sweet Madison had turned around just in time to see me sliding on my back like a teenage-mutant-ninja turtle down the stairs of the New York subway system. She screamed, "MAMA!" and ran down the stairs in total horror.

Then my adrenaline started to fall, and I started laughing hysterically—and I truly mean hysterically. I could see myself from afar – my legs sprawled in the air, a green duffel bag on my back – clearly looking like a turtle that had been flipped on its back and couldn't get up. As I started to laugh, Madison's look of horror turned to worry, and then a small smile crept over her face. I looked around me, still unable to right myself, as many New Yorkers promptly walked over and around me. No one stopped to help.

The next thing I heard was Mike's irritated voice yelling down to me, "WHAT IS TAKING YOU SO LONG?"

I was finally able to catch my breath and yell out, "HELP?"

That's when I saw his face peek around the corner of the stairs. I'm not sure what happened first – the look of absolute concern or the look of amusement. My gut tells me it was the look of concern first. But I was talking, so I must be okay! There I was—his 6'1" tall wife, with a green duffel bag on her back, and her arms and legs waving frantically above her looking very much like the turtle that she was trying desperately not to portray!

So he came down and helped me detangle myself from the mess that I was. Even with blood streaming down my flesh-torn hands, we still had a task to accomplish, and we still had a LONG way to go. So I pulled up my bootstraps, stood up, put on my fifty-pound duffel bag, grabbed the two other fifty pound duffel bags, and made my way to the top of those stairs. There was NO way I was going to be defeated by New York! And we were still only HALFWAY to our apartment.

More than an hour and a half after leaving the airport we finally arrived to our apartment.

The month in New York was intense, filled with language acquisition skills, cultural evaluation, public transportation, and figuring out how to live in a new place. These were all important skills that our mission agency wanted to impart to us prior to leaving for our mission field. All in all there were twenty-five new missionaries and their families that were being equipped to hit the field. We had finished all of our support raising, so this was the last stop for our family before we headed to Honduras.

"But by the grace of God I am what I am, and his grace toward me was not in vain. On the contrary, I worked harder than any of them, though it was not I, but the grace of God that is with me." - 1 Corinthians 15:10

Chapter 3

Sri Lanka

"Rejoice in hope, be patient in tribulation, be constant in prayer." – Romans 12:12

Boxing Day, 2004. A giant tsunami hit the island nations of the Indian Ocean, washing away 230,000 lives in one of the most devastating natural disasters in modern history. I wanted to be on the disaster team to respond, but I didn't have the vacation time nor the funds to get me there. My mother, who financially contributed to many humanitarian efforts, handed me a blank check to cover all my expenses, including the wages I would lose while I was gone. My parents were some of our first financial supporters when we went on the mission field; they loved us dearly and lived what they believed.

So in January 2005, only a few weeks after the awful events of the "Boxing Day Tsunami," I stepped off of a plane with my fellow disaster relief team mates onto the tarmac of Colombo, Sri Lanka. The air was humid; the atmosphere was chaotic. Planes were arriving and departing, the coastal waters were filled with cargo boats, ministry boats, and other relief efforts. For that matter, the streets were lined with boats, upside down cars, and much debris that had been brought in by the devastating wave that washed up on the shore.

We were met by a local church member who was going to be our guide and translator for our time in Sri Lanka. This was a surveillance trip. We wanted to know how future teams could be utilized here. I had brought along some medical equipment, but it really was for emergency purposes only. Our team consisted of a team leader, a counselor, a student in medical school, myself, and a few other team members there to help us coordinate our efforts. We wove our way through the multitudes of people coming to help and the morose crowd of people trying desperately to leave the country.

With no rest for the weary travelers, we set off. One of the first refugee/survivor camps we arrived in was a tent city that the UN or some other relief group had set up. Would future teams be of service here? Did we need medical groups to come, or was it going to be a group of construction workers, or a little bit of both? The needs were overwhelming. Food was in short supply, potable water all but non-existent. People were wandering aimlessly from tent to tent still seeking out lost family members. Soon after our arrival we sat down with some folks in the camp city. The hollow, lost look on most faces was haunting. We wanted to hear their stories. We wanted to understand their grief.

A gentleman in his early thirties sat down before us. He was wearing the same dirty clothing he wore on the day the tsunami hit. His eyes were hollow from grief and lack of sleep, his hair matted and encrusted with sea water, and his nails broken from the ordeal of trying to stay alive. He began telling us his story of that fateful day.

We were preparing our food and heard the strangest sound. It was like thunder, and yet it wasn't. It was like the earth was groaning, and we all looked at each other with confusion and wonder on our faces. We looked to the sea – what had been the oceanfront was gone. It was like the water was sucked away and the ocean was no longer lapping up on our shores. We knew something was wrong, we just didn't know what. How could we? We had no memory or stories from our fathers or our fathers' fathers that spoke of such things. It seemed like forever, but it also seemed so fast. The water was coming—it was coming as a wall to engulf our village. We screamed, we ran. What else was there to do? We ran fast, my wife, my child and myself. I grabbed my three-year-old so she wouldn't be caught up in the wave. My wife pulled up her ankle-length dress so she could run faster, but it was no use. The water was coming. I came upon a coconut tree and started climbing with my child on my back. I reached down for my wife who was desperately trying to climb up as well. In that moment, the wave struck.

With my wife's hand in my hand and my child on my back, we braced for the oncoming wave as it swept by us. My arm strained with the effort to keep my wife in my grasp. Her eyes looked at mine, and we both knew—we knew in that moment that it was our child or her life. So I let her go—I let her go, and she was dragged down by her heavy dress into the depths of the wave. I screamed in anger and frustration as I knew there was no hope for her survival – the wave was hungry for its victims.

I climbed higher into the coconut tree, and somehow managed to escape the onslaught of the force of the wave that had taken away our entire village and most of the lives of my neighbors. I clung to the tree, desperate to save myself, to save my child. How long I clung to the tree, I cannot even guess. Beneath me swirled dirty water filled with the sand it had churned up, dead animals that were unable to escape, and the fragments of our wood homes. It gradually receded, and I was able to climb down.

Set before me was a scene I couldn't have imagined even in my wildest dreams. I was not an educated man, but I knew about war. I knew the devastation that a bomb could make, and that's what it looked like. It looked like a bomb had exploded, leaving only the remnants of what used to be houses, trees, crops. But what was missing were the remains of people; there was no one left – everyone had been washed out to sea. An entire village – gone.

I lost my wife…I lost my wife…

His story ended with those haunting words. Tears flowed from his eyes as he remembered the horror that would likely haunt him for the rest of his life.

We sat in a circle, listening to the man's story. We were just a group of people, fellow human beings, who wanted to help the man feel his grief. A dear friend once told me, "You have to feel it to heal it." It would be a long time, I was sure, before this man would ever come to terms with what happened, if ever.

Knowing that the devastation was wide-spread, we continued on to another village. This time we were surrounded by children. These children that had survived the terror of The Wave, but their parents had not. They had been orphaned in mere moments. We didn't bring medicine, but we brought a taste of normalcy. Blank paper, color crayons, balloons, and time. We brought ourselves – no "mission" to accomplish, just ourselves. The kids came in droves. Without being asked, the majority of them drew pictures of the tsunami. They were drawing their experiences on paper, expressing what they couldn't put words to. It was an awe-inspiring moment. To share the heart of a child, and meet them where they were—we couldn't have done anything more important.

Then a woman approached us. She grasped the hand of a three-year-old who was walking beside her. They had found this young child wandering the shore hours after the tsunami. They didn't know who he was, where his family was, or where he had come from. He had stopped talking and woke up every night screaming from the terrors he witnessed. She brought him to us asking for help. We sat him down, and our counselor brought out a box filled with sand, plastic animals, and people. Given the opportunity to create, the child made a house out of sticks and put the plastic people inside the house. Then he smashed the house and stirred up the sand until there was nothing left. Next he put some plastic people walking toward a lone figure on the sand. He walked the little person toward the group of people, and he smiled. He was welcomed…he was taken in…he was an orphan who had found a new home. He looked up at us to see if we could see into his mind, and we all smiled down at him. He smiled in return and glanced up at the woman who had brought him. Then he jumped up, ran to her, and hugged her. The woman could only look down at the child and hug him back. He had "spoken" although he said no words. And he had been heard.

> *"When you pass through the waters, I will be with you; and through the rivers, they shall not overwhelm you; when you walk through fire you shall not be burned, and the flame shall not consume you." – Isaiah 43:2*

Chapter 4

Honduras

"For this I toil, struggling with all his energy that he powerfully works within me." - Colossians 1:29

My family and I made the trek to Honduras the summer of 2008, after almost a year of studying Spanish in Costa Rica. We came as the first in country from our mission sending organization. We arrived in country alone—with no one to greet us at the airport. Of the 16 bags that were supposed to arrive with us, only two showed up—and one of those was a guitar. So, we grabbed our two bags, got into a taxi, and headed toward town. We had heard about a home that was rented out to people on a limited basis, so we headed in that direction. Gratefully, we were able to make the arrangements and set ourselves up in this tiny little flat where we would stay for the next three weeks while we looked for a house to rent.

Within a month of our arrival, we had our first short-term team visit. It was a medical team. We headed to a community we had looked at—a little village called Armenia Bonito. It was a 3,000- person village of fairly poor people. Most cooked on outside fire pits. Everyone within the community either hand washed their clothes in a sink outside of their house or walked to the river to wash their clothes. Most houses did not have running water, and residents used a latrine outside of their house. Since this was the community that my husband and I had considered working long-term, this was where we brought the medical brigade.

The brigade was a success and provided us an introduction to the community. Trying to be good little missionaries, we didn't want to start any programs or do anything without really getting a good feel of the community. So the next several weeks we spent going door-to-door and just talking to people. What were the needs of the home? What kind of programs did they want to see started? It gave us a chance to see how people lived day-to-day and what the average age and occupancy of each home was.

Shortly after that we started an English class, a children's program, and a weekly medical clinic. We still were without a car, so this meant we walked to the bus stop nearest our house, caught the bus, and took the LONG ride out to the community. All told, it took about an hour and a half each way to get to Armenia Bonito. We had to coordinate our timing as we needed to get our daughter to school in the morning and then be able to pick her up at the end of the day.

English class was a huge hit. We had so many people within the community show up. Then, after class ended, I opened up my medical bag and prepared to do a medical clinic…except no one showed. We had done tons of advertising and talked to people in their homes, but no one came. My heart sank.

With 13 years of experience working in a pediatric hospital and having taught childbirth education classes for almost twenty years, I definitely felt that I had something that I could share. I had tried to equip myself by attending some seminars and tropical medicine courses. In addition, I read whatever I could get my hands on to try and prepare me to be a "jungle nurse." In my mind, I knew what that looked like, but I didn't know how the reality was going to pan out.

David said to Gad, "I am in deep distress. Let us fall into the hands of the Lord, for his mercy is great; but do not let me fall into human hands." – 2 Samuel 24:14

Chapter 5

What am I Worth?
A Nurse on the Mission Field

"Fear not, therefore; you are of more value than many sparrows." - Matthew 10:31

When we went on the mission field, I gave up my calling as a pediatric oncology nurse to work in the field of public health instead. I DAILY wondered what I was doing. What difference was I making? Had I changed a life? Had I saved a life? Had I made a difference? It's what we were here to do, after all.

Hard work is ingrained in my nature. I started working and making money at fifteen-and-a-half years old, the earliest you could obtain a work permit in the state of California. Since that time my work experience has been broad: fast food, cashier, U.S. Army, secretary, waitress, and nurse. The only time I didn't work was the three months after my daughter Madison was born. I was successful at what I did. I felt accomplished. I made great money. Then we went to the mission field. I no longer made ANY money.

I got my work ethic from my parents, who were both self-starters. My mother grew up in an extremely poor family in Central Valley, California. She moved out of her parents' home right after high school and went to San Jose, where she received her degree from Santa Clara University, becoming one of the first woman managers in a computer firm well before computer firms were even a "thing." She met my dad, they fell in love, and history was made. My dad was my step-dad, but to me, he was the only thing that mattered. He was the man who helped mold me, raise me, and make me into the woman I am now.

My parents instilled in me the value of taking care of myself. I joined the Army to pay my way through school. My parents certainly had the funds to pay my way through all my years in college, but that was not their way. They wanted me to find my own path. So the Army it was. At seventeen, I drove down to the Army recruiter and spent the afternoon talking to him. By the end of the conversation, I knew what I wanted to do. I talked to my mom, who needed to sign the "okay" for me to join the Army (as I was underage), and my path was set. A few weeks after graduating high school I set out for boot camp.

Although my parents loved the United States, they were not all that patriotic. They never instilled in me what it was to be an American. I gained that love all by myself. I'm not sure why, but there you have it. I cry when I hear the National Anthem. I taught my daughter all the historical facts of the United States along with all the songs to go with them. She saluted the United States flag every day when we home schooled, and she led her Honduran schoolmates in the National Anthem of the United States. I was a proud American...I am STILL a proud American. The U.S. Army gave me the means to make it through college.

My first week in boot camp, the drill sergeant looked at me and saw something—he saw what my potential could be. I was assigned to be platoon leader for our group, and I led the way. I graduated boot camp with high marks and moved on to my Advanced Training.

It was 1986, the middle of the Cold War, and war was a reality. I worked in a Patriot Missile System unit as a radio transmit operator, encrypting and decrypting messages from higher to lower echelon units. I was stationed in Hanau, Germany, and our unit patrolled active air space between East and West Germany. We spent two weeks of every six in the forest of Germany preparing for war.

When all was said and done, after my three years in Germany, I returned to the States where I spent another six years in an active Reserve MASH unit while finishing Nursing School at CSU Sacramento. It was there I met my future husband.

With a girlfriend who had spent time in Cold War Germany, my husband felt a call to military service as well. His father was a World War II vet, serving 32 years in the former Army Air Corp, the predecessor of today's Air Force. My future husband had been denied entry into the Marines because of his flat feet, but after meeting me, he tried again and was admitted into the U.S. Army where we served together in the MASH unit, even going to Jump School together.

When I graduated nursing school, the majority of jobs I looked for clearly stated: *New nurses need not apply.* It took me six months of full-time searching to find a job. While I was in nursing school, I worked full-time as a secretary in a state job. This gave me priority when searching for state jobs. After unsuccessfully applying for hospital jobs for six months, I applied for a job at a juvenile detention center.

My stories of my time there could take up another whole book, but suffice it to say, I learned many skills that would take me a long way in the "real" world. When I started nursing school I had no idea what field of nursing I was interested in. However, while studying both pediatric nursing and OB/GYN nursing, it became clear where my passion lay. My attempts to try to work in labor and delivery were denied over and over, until I finally looked at a pediatric department. I finally was hired at an incredible children's hospital, where I strove day in and day out to save the lives of children burdened with the awful disease of cancer.

All of these experiences prepared me to face the harsh realities of the mission field. My husband, daughter and I were going through this adventure together. We had our experience to back us, and we knew we could take this adventure on. Yet here I was, in Honduras, facing a whole other level of *I-have-no-idea-what-I'm-doing* kind of work. Walking through the streets of the village where we were serving, we often times wondered if we were making a difference.

Being a mom, wife, and missionary has always been a challenge. I came to the field as a "professional" woman, having had a full-time career (working nights) so I could be a full-time mom as well. I homeschooled my daughter and never missed an activity or event she was in. I spent days sleep-deprived to raise my child in a home full of love and inclusiveness. I didn't want her to "suffer" because her mom worked full-time. So I continued to work night shifts well after my body said "enough" and well after the numerous day shift positions were filled by others who had less experience than me. I wanted to be there for my child. It was the best of both worlds!

But on the mission field—and sometimes in the States as well—women live in a terrible dichotomy. Our culture tells us to be accomplished. Our female peers who have jobs look at us and judge us based on what we do for a living. On the other hand, our friends who are stay-at-home moms look at us and shake their heads that we are taking away precious time from our children and working instead. It is a hard place to be—this place of mom/wife/career woman. We are never fully accepted by those who are only one or the other.

Then the mission field—the working mom comes to the field and is torn. Do you commit yourself to your family? Do you commit yourself to being a missionary? Or are you able to do a little of both? Will you be judged by those moms who are choosing to be at home with their family? What about those that are working full-time as missionaries?

I chose to be both. I was a full-time missionary nurse and a full-time mom. It came easily to me. It's what I did before the mission field, so being able to work and be a wife and mom at the same time was very natural. But now I did it for free. As a volunteer, I worked full-time as a nurse but made no money. I certainly didn't have a normal job as a nurse. I was the Director for Medical/Mercy Ministry for our team in La Ceiba. I organized mobile medical clinics at all the sites we had missionaries working in. I organized and ran the medical brigades that we brought in 3-4 times a year. I ultimately opened a permanent medical clinic in the jungles of Honduras, hired a Honduran physician and a Honduran nurse, and oversaw the clinic. It was a full-time job, no doubt. But I felt like I was not contributing to my family. I had been working since I was 15½ years old. For that entire time I brought money to the table. I contributed. I mattered. Now I didn't.

I didn't realize I felt any of this until we returned to the States on furlough and I got a job as a nurse at a children's hospital. I once again made really good money. I was contributing to the family. I felt accomplished! I was able to pay cash to get Madison, our daughter, to Europe during the summer for overseas study for her college. We paid off our bills, were able to go out to eat whenever we wanted, had date nights out, and lived a little freely with the extra money I was making. I didn't find myself having to transfer money from Mike's account to mine—I had my own money. It felt great! I won't deny it. But this brought to the surface feelings I didn't even realize I had. What is it that gives me a sense of purpose? What is it that makes me feel accomplished? Where do I find my satisfaction?

Now I am NOT talking about the satisfaction of who I am in Christ. I have always felt that whatever I do, I do for the glory of God. That if I follow where He leads, there is no wrong. That He can use a weak vessel, like me, to accomplish what He wants. So what is it? I had to dig deeper to find the source and origin of my anxiety. Then it dawned on me—it's my culture. The culture I grew up in showed me the only way I was successful was to be accomplished in a career.

When I applied for my position at the children's hospital during furlough, they didn't even contact our mission agency. They didn't view my work on the mission field as "work" at all. They wanted to know the last hospital I was employed at—because that was actual work, and mission work wasn't work. Don't get me wrong—as an agency that cares for sick children in a hospital setting, they wanted to see how I had worked with sick children in a hospital setting. I get it—but it also highlighted the fact that our own culture doesn't value what we do as missionaries. In the eyes or our culture, during our time on the mission field I had been without a job, and the IRS confirmed that—I had no reportable income for those seven years.

So here is my confession: this is my struggle. I struggle when visiting nurses and doctors come down to my clinic and see where I work. I see that in some of their eyes what I do is not "real" nursing. The medical profession is a tough field. More often than not nurses can eat their young. We want titles and initials behind our names. When I am told, "Oh, we don't do it like that anymore" (in hospitals in the U.S.)—it stings. I feel like I'm so behind the curve and less of a nurse.

That maybe I don't matter anymore. I know—I know—pride is such an evil thing! The root of most of our sin.

The bottom line is—why does it matter what I look like in other people's eyes? I am following God's calling for me, and He is the only one I matter to. The thing that speaks to my heart is that when I stand before Him on my final day and He looks at me, the ONLY thing I long to hear is, "Well done...my good and faithful servant," because I followed Him.

And the King will answer them, 'Truly, I say to you, as you did it to one of the least of these my brothers, you did it to me.' - Matthew 25:40

Then I heard the voice of the Lord, saying, "Whom shall I send, and who will go for Us?" Then I said, "Here am I. Send me!" - Isaiah 6:8

"For I know the plans I have for you, declares the Lord, plans for welfare and not for evil, to give you a future and a hope." - Jeremiah 29:11

Chapter 6

The Baby

"Beloved, I pray that all may go well with you and that you may be in good health, as it goes well with your soul." – 3 John 1:2

No one was going to come to my clinics, I would try a different angle. I would hold a pregnancy clinic. The average age of a first-time pregnancy in Honduras is fifteen years old. I knew that I would have plenty of young women that would come.

So, the following week I walked around the community handing out flyers and talking to people, telling them to please come to the clinic. I could do an exam on them, check their blood pressure and blood sugar, and give them prenatal vitamins. Surely many people women would come.

Two showed up. I was once again disappointed, but I would be the BEST provider I could be for my two little patients. I saw the first— measured her belly, listened to the baby's heart beat with my fetoscope, talked to her about her pregnancy and what to expect during delivery, and asked her to return once she had the baby so that I could assess her baby. She agreed.

The second pregnant mom came and sat down. I recognized her— it was the woman I had seen in the village the week before whom I had begged to come. She was not a big woman, but her belly looked truly enormous. Gratefully, she heeded my request and came. Before I did anything, we talked. I asked her about her family, how long she had lived in the community, if she worked, etc. Then came the assessment. I asked her to lie down, and I attempted to measure her belly. She didn't know when her last menstrual cycle had been, not even a guesstimate. So, I didn't have much to go on other than the size of her uterus to try and determine gestational age. So, I measured…and measured again… and measured again. I was getting over 50 centimeters. A good rough rule of thumb is that fundal height, when expressed in centimeters, roughly corresponds to gestational age in weeks between 16 and 36 weeks for a vertex baby. So there was NO way that 50 centimeters was anything but not good. I must stress that this was not a big woman. She was average to small build, but her belly…I couldn't wrap my brain around it. I asked her—was she pregnant with twins?

"NO WAY!" she said.

I asked her if she was SURE she wasn't pregnant with twins, to which she replied, "I have 11 other children. I think I would KNOW if I was pregnant with twins."

Okay. So I took her blood pressure...and took it again on the other arm to make sure, but the common reading I was getting was 220/110. I looked at her hands and feet—sure enough—swollen. I asked her if she had headaches, to which she replied yes. Any nausea or vomiting? Yes, she replied. Okay… NOT good… all signs of preeclampsia.

I asked her if she had had anything to eat or drink that morning, and she said she only had some water. Great—I could check a fasting blood sugar on her. So, I did... then I checked it again… then I got my "back-up" machine and checked it again… 450. Anywhere from 70 – 100 is a good fasting blood sugar—hers was 450. Her belly made sense—she had gestational diabetes.

Her blood sugar, her blood pressure, and all her signs said this was an emergency. She needed to go to the hospital immediately. I did my best to explain what was going on. I explained the reason behind her headaches, swelling, nausea, and her VERY big belly. I told her she needed to go to the hospital NOW! I realized that when I said this, I was telling her a lot of things. I was telling her she needed to leave her other children at home. I was telling her that she needed to ride the bus forty-five minutes to get to the hospital. I realized that I was telling her she had to take money, because she was going to have to pay to be seen. I realized all of this knowing the probability of her going was very slim. She was angry. She did not trust me. She looked at me and said she was going to go home and have her baby at home like she had had all of her other eleven babies before, and who was I to tell her what to do? I begged. I pleaded. I told her that if she wanted to live to be around to care for her other children, she needed to go to the hospital now. She looked at me, said a few choice words, and walked out – back in the direction of her home.

Tears welled up in my eyes. What in the world was I thinking? I am JUST a nurse! I can't do this! Who do I think I am? I can't make a difference! This woman could very well stroke out, have a seizure, bleed out—all sorts of things, and I couldn't stop it from happening. I got on the bus to go home. I sat and gazed out the window, looking at people and cars passing by. I wondered why I was here. What could just a nurse do? I was haunted by her back as she turned and walked away.

Two days later I was back out in the village making house calls when a young girl came running up to me. "JUST COME!" she said, and ran off, so I followed her. And where did I end up? At the house of the same mom who had stormed off from my clinic just two days prior – and what was she holding in her hands? Her new baby. She looked at me and confessed her anger. She said that she went home and thought about what I had told her. She thought about being around for the rest of her children, and the possibility of not making it. She made arrangements with a neighbor to watch her other children, walked house to house collecting money she knew she would need upon her arrival at the hospital, and she went. She told me that the hospital was irritated with her because she wasn't in active labor. The hospital only admits pregnant moms if they are at least five centimeters dilated. It doesn't matter if you have traveled far and have no place to stay, they will assess you and send you out if you are not five centimeters dilated. But she explained to them what I had told her. She said that an American doctor had told her to come. No matter how many times I've tried to tell people to call me nurse, I am referred to as Doctora Teresa, my middle name, which is easier for Spanish speakers.

With irritation and an attitude (her words), they took her in to at least assess her, with the full intention of turning her away—until they checked her blood pressure and blood sugar. Within thirty minutes they had her in the OR getting ready for a cesarean. The mom placed her fourteen-pound newborn baby on my lap with tears streaming down her face. I looked at this precious, smiling baby in my lap, with a head full of hair, and looked back up at this sweet mama, and my tears came as well.

"You saved me. You saved me and my baby."

I could only smile and praise sweet Jesus who had moved this mama to come see me at clinic, then moved her to go to the hospital to have her baby.

So I—just a nurse—had made a difference. And a new life had arrived and survived.

Here she is holding one of the flyers I made for the pregnancy clinic.

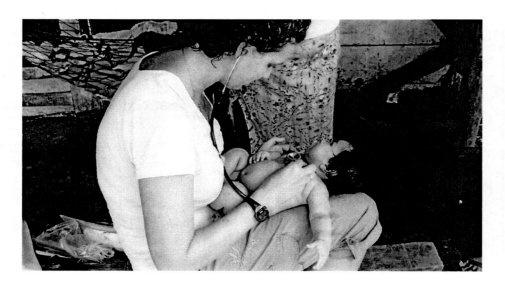

Here I am assessing her brand-new, two-day-old, fourteen-pound baby.

But in your great mercy you did not put an end to them or abandon them, for you are a gracious and merciful God. – Nehemiah 9:31

Chapter 7

Justin

"But when you give a feast, invite the poor, the crippled, the lame, the blind, and you will be blessed, because they cannot repay you. For you will be repaid at the resurrection of the just." -Luke 14:13-14

After the diabetic mother's experience with my pregnancy clinic, people started to trust me. Word got out that maybe I really did know what I was doing. My weekly clinics started blossoming. I would show up and have upwards of 85-100 people waiting for me. It got to a point where I would have to hand out numbers because it was just little ol' me, and there was no way I could see that many people.

Medical Brigades were another way to reach out to new communities as well. Branching out into communities by offering medical clinics was a great way to bring people in. By this time, several long-term and short-term missionaries joined our team. We were no longer alone. So, once a week I would rotate mobile clinics into two additional villages where we had long-term missionaries on our team serving. There were two advantages to this. We were able to offer many more services to the folks in these areas, and it allowed the medical brigades to experience different communities—a win-win situation indeed.

One such brigade brought us to a riverside community called La Fe (The Faith). This medical brigade was unique in that it brought an optometrist – the first one we had had. A year earlier I had been given about 300 pairs of glasses by a local chapter of the Rotary Club. Each pair of glasses was carefully marked with the prescription so that someone who knew what they were doing could assess a patient and provide a pair of glasses that closely fit their needs. This is a huge benefit for very poor patients who not only can't afford to get an eye exam, but then certainly can't afford to buy glasses if they need them. The line to see our optometrist went around the block! Once again, I had to hand out numbers and turn many many people away because we simply didn't have enough time to see them all.

Towards the end of the day, a mother approached me with her five children. She not only wanted them to be seen by the pediatrician, but she also wanted her five-year-old son to be seen by the optometrist. I looked at this little boy running around playing and thought, *No way! He doesn't need glasses!* But the mom looked at me, and the look in her eyes spoke differently.

Typically, I am not moved by pleading eyes. I can't be. I have to have a partial barrier between me and the needy. I learned this self-preservation when I worked as a pediatric oncology nurse for twelve years. I am empathetic, caring, nurturing and efficient; but I can't emotionally attach to every child because to do so would be devastating. I couldn't do my job. During my time there we lost many children that we had cared for for years. It is a heartache each and every time, and sometimes can make your job impossible. So, you have to set a little part of your heart aside so you can continue to do your job.

It was no different, I was finding, in Honduras. The needs are overwhelming, the poverty severe, the medical conditions great. But being able to help means having to set limits, and that means turning people away who really need to be seen so that you can focus on those you can actually care for.

So when this mom turned her pleading eyes to me, I typically would not have been swayed to change my mind, but something nudged me. Against my better judgment, I gave her a number.

I walked over to our optometrist and explained to him the situation. I assured him that my normal MO was NOT to cave in to every sad pair of eyes, but something had told me otherwise. I asked him if he could see this boy. Yes, he agreed. The boy would be the last one, but we needed to see if we had time to get him in before we left.

When I saw that Justin, this little five-year old, was going to be the next and last patient, I walked over to our optometrist to give him my thanks. After assessing this little guy, the doc looked at me with wide open eyes. He said, "I don't know how this boy even sees. He's basically blind! All he must be able to see is color and shapes."

My eyebrows went up. Really? He was running around and playing.

"Yes," the doc said, "He has learned how to compensate and live in his mostly blind world."

"So, what can we do for this little guy?" I asked. The doc walked over to where the 300 pairs of glasses were and started searching. He searched, and searched, and searched. He finally gave the age-old shout of victory—EUREKA! He pulled out what looked like a 1970's women's pair of thick, pop-bottle glasses. They were HUGE! I just knew when we put them on his little face that they would be bigger than him. But we called Justin over and placed the glasses on his face. The look of wonder and sheer joy that erupted from this little face will never leave my memory. The grin that stretched from ear to ear was catching! We all started smiling, then laughing at his sheer joy!

My friend asked him in Spanish, "Justin, how many fingers am I holding up?"

With the confidence of a boy five times his age, but with the exuberance of a five-year-old, he started jumping up and down, clapping his hands, and in amazement and wonder said,

"You have TWO! YOU HAVE TWO?"

Amazing Grace!—how sweet the sound—that saved a wretch like me! I once was lost, but now am found, was blind, but now I see.

"But he said to me, "My grace is sufficient for you, for my power is made perfect in weakness." Therefore I will boast all the more gladly of my weaknesses, so that the power of Christ may rest upon me." - 2 Corinthians 12:9

Chapter 8

The Flood

"In the six hundred and first year, in the first month, the first day of the month, the waters were dried from off the earth. And Noah removed the covering of the ark and looked, and behold, the face of the ground was dry."—*Genesis 8:13*

Every Thursday before we had our permanent clinic, my husband, our interns, and I would pack up my little red truck full of medication, supplies, tables, and chairs, and head out to the little village of Armenia Bonito. It was rainy season, so we weren't all that surprised that a slight rain had begun to fall. Our daughter was safely at school for the day, and we sped away in the truck. To get to the village by bus took a good hour and a half: all the little side communities and single lane roads really didn't allow for a much quicker trip. However, in our little truck we could get there in about twenty-five minutes.

We were less than five minutes into our drive when the heavens opened. Now, we were not ones to let a little rain stop us—we did live in a rain forest country after all. Our little town got about 132 inches of rain a year, so a good-sized downpour was not completely unheard of. However, this was different. Not even five more minutes into our trip, the water had filled all the side streets and was rushing sideways over the road we were on. Still not realizing the full severity of what we were encountering, we continued on to the village.

Along the road by the village we worked in there was a fairly big river. Most of the time it was easily less than half full. The city we lived in was located at the base of a huge mountain range. When big

39

storms came in, they hit that mountain range and stopped. The jungle was flooded with water, and the huge river drained it off into the ocean only a few miles away.

On this day, however, as we drove by the river, the water from the river was less than a foot from our tires. We looked at each other and knew that clinic was canceled for the day, and our trip was all but at an end. We at least wanted to make sure the people in the village were safe. So we drove on for about the next half-mile, when the water on the road started to come up over the top of our tires, and we knew we were in trouble. We made it into the village, but the bridge we needed to cross was flooded over with water. We saw a few people running around. We asked how everyone was doing, and over the thundering noise of the pounding rain they yelled back that everyone was okay for now. So, before we got stuck, we put the truck in reverse and slowly made our way out of the village.

By the time we drove back into the city, there was chaos everywhere. If there was a community on the side of the road that was lower than street level, it was flooded out—some more than halfway up. We tried to contact our daughter's school, but all the cell lines were down. And then it happened—we got stuck. Our car wouldn't move. The water was now above the bottom part of our doors. I rolled the window down so I could climb out. While my husband took care of the car, one of the interns and I were going to walk to the school to collect my daughter.

I jumped out into the street, with the water about midway up my thigh, and we started trudging in the direction of my daughter's school. To walk the distance to her school (less than a mile), it took us well over an hour. Slogging our way through the water, with the rain still pouring down, we finally made it to the community right near her school. Just then an electric utility truck came down the street. They motioned for us to jump on the back of the truck, and they took us the rest of the way.

When we pulled up to the school and my eleven-year-old daughter saw me walking toward her, the relief that flooded her little body was palpable. She hoisted her backpack, full of books, on top of her head and started wading out in our direction.

The reunion was sweet! We hugged and laughed and cried at the absurdity of the entire situation. And then we started the long trek back to the car. The rain had started to slow by this point, and the water to slowly recede. By the time we made it back to the car, where my anxious husband was waiting, it had receded enough to allow us to drive the remaining half-mile home.

Over the next few days, we hosted a number of refugees from flooded communities. We even got a phone call from some friends of ours that were up in the mountains. Their entire community had been cut off from the city by the flooded river. All of the tiny little shops around their town had quickly run out of food. So we ran to the grocery store and filled our car full of rice, beans, flour, milk, oil, toilet paper, diapers, and formula—as much as it could hold—and drove to one side of the swollen river. Our friend had managed to secure a small boat, and he met us on our side of the river. We unloaded all of the supplies, and he rowed the boat back over to the other side, loaded up his truck, and drove the precious cargo back to his community where it would be shared.

This was no hurricane or tropical storm, just a bad weather front that had quickly moved in and then moved out just as quickly. But in the three hours it had stayed, the entire city was turned upside down. Once again, because of the limited resources and infrastructure in Honduras, the people were on their own. There would be no rescue units coming, no supply trucks or refugee tents set up. Communities pulled together, and everyone helped one another.

"Finally, all of you, be like-minded, be sympathetic, love one another, be compassionate and humble."—Mark 12:31

Chapter 9

This is the House that God Built

"By wisdom a house is built, and by understanding it is established;"—Proverbs 24:3

My house in the States was comfortable, no question about it. It was a two-story home with three bedrooms, two-and-a-half bathrooms, a living room and dining room, and a beautiful back yard complete with a swimming pool. Our garage could easily store our two cars, three motorcycles, and still had storage space for "stuff." My kitchen was a "normal" kind of kitchen. It had a nice refrigerator, stove and oven, dish washer, double sink and counter space to be able to prepare my meals. I was able to work in my house at the computer in seventy-two degree temperature year-round as my heater kicked on during the winter and my air conditioner during the summer. We lived in what I would consider an average kind of home.

I would ask you to think in your mind what your own home looks like. What is your favorite room? What new carpeting or hardwood floor have you recently installed? Do you have a fireplace or a den where you work on your computer in the evening?

Now I ask you to take a moment and put yourself in a different home. Imagine living in a 200-square-foot shack with wall boards that don't meet, so insects and critters can come and go. I ask you to think about those really stormy days where the rain is pounding down on your roof, but your roof is rusted tin that keeps almost nothing dry. As you get ready to prepare your lunch, you must first go to the forest and collect wood, then start the campfire outside of your home and cook whatever you have with the single pot you own. Then as the sun sets and you have no electricity to turn on any lights, you settle yourself down on a bed that lies underneath a lean-to with only a small roof overhead—no walls, no floor, nothing to protect you from the elements or critters that roam in the night. When you get up the next morning, you must go to the river to get your water for the day—the water you use to bathe, wash your clothing, clean dishes, etc.

I hope you have taken the time to put these images into your head, because I would like to introduce you to Alejandro. Alejandro is a humble, sweet man who has experienced a lot in his life. It's worth taking the time to listen to his story. This seventy-six-year-old man lost his wife more than twenty-five years ago, has never remarried, and has no children. He daily goes into the jungle to cut down trees with his machete and bring them into the village to sell for small change. There is no electricity in his home and no running water; he cooks over a camp fire; and his little wooden shack is too small to even hold his bed, so his bed is on the back side of his house covered by a lean-to made of sticks with a tin covering to keep it from the rain.

Alejandro's small, simple house…

One of the things we wanted to do in Armenia Bonito was to get involved in people's lives. We had made the decision to never hand out money. We didn't want to be the local Santa Claus; we wanted to make a difference in people's lives through acts of service, mercy ministry, and fellowship. One way we felt we could make a sincere difference in this man's life was to build him a house.

Summer teams were a way we could provide the money, manpower, and time to get this accomplished. So we started building and by the end of the summer, we had a new little house for Alejandro. It was the first house he had had in his entire life. His bed fit in nicely, we had electricity and plumbing put in, and he could sleep at night without the fear of a downpour or critters bothering him in the night.

"Therefore everyone who hears these words of mine and puts them into practice is like a wise man who built his house on the rock. The rain came down, the streams rose, and the winds blew and beat against that house; yet it did not fall, because it had its foundation on the rock. But everyone who hears these words of mine and does not put them into practice is like a foolish man who built his house on sand. The rain came down, the streams rose, and the winds blew and beat against that house, and it fell with a great crash."—Matthew 7:24-27

Chapter 10

The Mangled Leg

"But if anyone has the world's goods and sees his brother in need, yet closes his heart against him, how does God's love abide in him?"—1 John 3:17

When you live in a country where you have experienced the lack of resources and many pointless and preventable deaths, it is easy to see why people who have lived there their entire lives have a fatalistic view of life. Cancer is considered a "rich man's disease" where the average person could never hope for treatment. Cataracts steal the vision of countless people every day, with no hope of surgery. A life of fully intact teeth is a pipe dream. A premature baby is all but a death sentence. "Hope" seems like a faraway word. So, people in situations like this understand, in their hearts, that life is short. I saw the reality of this up close and personal one night.

My husband and I were sitting down to watch a movie on TV. Our daughter had already excused herself to go upstairs to her room and work on some art work on her computer. Suddenly she came running down the stairs. "Mom...MOM!" she said, "Someone is outside screaming for help!"

I jumped up, grabbed my emergency bag, and charged outside. My level-headed husband shouted, "STOP!"

I looked at him like, WHAT?

"This IS Honduras, after all, let me check it out first."

And of course, he was right. Living in the murder capital of the world, you do live life a little differently. You figure out how to maneuver through life as safely as possible, and you certainly don't go out after dark. It was dark—about ten at night. So, Mike walked out to our ten-foot-tall fence lined with razor wire, and assessed the situation. He saw about thirty people who had formed a circle around a man who was lying underneath his motorcycle. He looked up and down the street, ensuring that this wasn't a set-up for people lying in wait, and then gave me the "all clear."

We unlocked the front gate, and out I ran. I looked down at the man, who was without a helmet. He was covered by his motorcycle, with blood slowly spilling out. I looked at the people standing in a circle.

"Help me move the motorcycle!" I shouted at the people around me.

They looked at me like I was crazy, and each one of them took a step back. I knew the law. I knew that until police had arrived and assessed the situation for fault, nothing could be moved. But, seriously?! This was clearly different! There was a wounded man underneath that motorcycle!

In Spanish I yelled, "I'm a nurse, I can help! Help me get this motorcycle off!"

No one moved. I repeated the plea again. Still no one moved. I was angry—the kind of angry that pools at the underbelly of a normally calm and collected person, that only needs the right kind of trigger to erupt. And erupt it did. I was pissed! They seriously were going to wait for the police to arrive to help this man? Not a chance. With adrenaline pumping, I shoved the small-sized motorcycle off of the bleeding man. No one stepped in to help, but no one stopped me either. I think they didn't quite know what to do with this crazy gringa armed with only a medical bag.

I looked down at the conscious man and started talking to him, while at the same time looking for the source of blood, putting on my gloves, and getting my bandages ready. He talked to me in a coherent voice. I was grateful for this, as his helmet was nowhere to be found. He was oriented to time and place, knew his name and where he lived. All good signs. As I looked for the source of blood, it soon became very apparent his primary external source of injury. His leg was turned at more than a ninety-degree angle between his knee and hip. I felt through his untorn pants to feel a clearly compound femur fracture. The seriousness of this couldn't be understated. The femur, which is the strongest bone in the body, is surrounded by major sources of blood— the femoral artery being the primary one. I could see blood pooling around his leg. Trying to discern if it was arterial bleeding, I grabbed my pair of bandage scissors and cut away his pants.

At the same time I was yelling to people around me, asking if anyone had called for an ambulance. The only ambulance service in the city is a private service for which payment for services rendered is due beforehand, thank you very much. The response I got was that they had called, but no one had answered the phone. So, I then asked if the fire department had been called. Someone started calling. There are no medical personnel attached to a fire truck in Honduras, but I figured at least they could transport him to the public hospital. They also told me that the police were on the way.

So I cut away his pant leg and was thankful to not see spurting blood, and not the bright blood typical of arterial bleeding. However, there was still a substantial amount of bleeding. Grabbing my bandages, I was able to place an ABD bandage and some kerlix over the wound and substantially slow the rate of blood loss.

Then, to my relief, the fire department arrived. The firefighters casually got down from their engine, took out their stretcher, and calmly walked over to the man on the ground. I gave them a narrative of what had transpired, along with the patient's level of consciousness, etc.—all the things a receiving medical provider would want, but was quickly dismissed. They weren't medical personnel, and most of the information I passed on to them they didn't know what to do with. They all stood around the man, contemplating how they were going to move him. Finally, they asked a few of the men that were standing by if they would help. Without any consideration for or stabilization of his leg, they lifted him up and put him on the stretcher. I desperately tried to immobilize his leg while he was being lifted into the fire truck, but as they were more interested in getting him in the truck, I was only barely successful.

They tucked him in, and away they went. Off to the public hospital, I presume—that's the best he would get. I don't know what happened to the man—if he survived the ordeal, if his leg was spared, or if financial strain and convenience required an amputation (which is what I suspect happened). I never found out his fate.

But I was confronted with the harsh reality of what it was to live here. To go to a hospital that does not have a functioning x-ray machine, to have surgery performed with only local anesthesia as there is no mechanism for general anesthesia. Where surgery requires the up-front payment of all services, and family members are given a list of supplies to go out and purchase prior to surgery, includes gloves, gauze, IV fluids, tubing, medication, even gowns for the surgeons. I knew the probability of this man having his leg salvaged was slim to none.

The social injustices of medical care in third world countries can be overwhelming. But again, I was there to try and make a difference, however small it might be. Perhaps I helped to at least save the man's life by bandaging his leg and slowing his life's blood from seeping into the pavement beneath him. To be the only person—a foreigner—to talk to him and comfort him and to offer him aid. To be Christ's hands and feet as best I could—a stranger in a strange land.

"And great crowds came to him, bringing with them the lame, the blind, the crippled, the mute, and many others, and they put them at his feet, and he healed them,"—Matthew 15:30-31

Chapter 11

Oneida

"Let no corrupting talk come out of your mouths, but only such as is good for building up, as fits the occasion, that it may give grace to those who hear."—Ephesians 4:29

I wanted to do something fun and totally different for the girls in the community. I wanted a day to be all about them. In the community we worked in, there was an average of ten people per household. This meant that young ones were caring for even younger ones. Too often the nine-year-old is responsible for caring for the newborn baby in the house. With the average age of fifteen for a first-time pregnancy and a "love them and leave them" culture, there were many households where five to eight children were the norm.

I looked around the community and thought, *What about a day of just having fun? A day to pamper the young girls of the community.* This would be a girls' day out. We would primp and pamper girls who had never had an opportunity to be primped and pampered. I hired some hair dressers in the city that agreed to cut hair in the river. I solicited from churches in the States for hair ties, ribbons, shampoo, conditioner, soaps, etc. The gifts rained in. Boxes and boxes of supplies came in. Our interns and I spent weeks preparing goody bags filled with ribbons, hair ties, lotion, shampoo, conditioner, and nail polish for our girls.

We planned for a day of pampering. We would have a station to wash and delouse hair in the river, then send the newly washed girls over to the hair dressers where they would receive a professional haircut. They would then go to the next station and get their hair styled with ribbons and hair ties. After that was the station for nail polishing and glitter. In the end, they would receive a bag full of the supplies that we had been sent—their own personal bag of beauty supplies.

Oneida was a young girl whom we met not long after we arrived in Armenia Bonito. In the beginning days, she would look at us from afar, curious but afraid to approach. We would see her watching us, safely from a distance, but with a clear longing on her face to be involved. But we just couldn't get her to trust us.

We slowly started learning about her, and she became dear to our hearts. Oneida was mute. For all intents and purposes she didn't speak. She had learned to mimic a few sounds to try and make herself understood, but had no grasp of her own language. She was not deaf and understood when you spoke to her. Her mother died when she was quite young, but no one really knew the story of what happened. Her father was a day worker and was gone from the house for most of the day, but even when he was home, he gave almost no care or attention to Oneida, her sister, or her brother. So Oneida was alone in caring for her small family.

Over several months, she slowly started approaching these funny-looking white people. She was fearful, and we found out why. She was the local "beating block"—if someone was frustrated or angry and Oneida was nearby, she became the brunt of their fury and was beat upon.

However, when Oneida saw the pampering day activities going on and the safety with all the other girls around, she came. She wanted her hair cut, and for us to put pretty bows in her hair. She clung desperately to the goody bag we had given her, showing anyone who would look the gifts she had received that day. From that day on she decided that we were safe adults. From that time on, she looked upon us as people who loved her. She came to every activity we put on—from English classes to helping out in medical clinic, and every Kids Club.

My daughter on my left, and Oneida on my right.

Eventually, we were able to build a house for her little family and provide a safe place for her to sleep. One of the last houses we visited before we left Honduras was the house of Oneida and her family. We brought a food basket, clothing, blankets, and love. We told them of our plans to leave Honduras and move to Africa, and of our love for them. We hugged them, prayed for them, and left them in God's care. Helping the least…in that we were so bountifully blessed.

"He gives power to the faint, and to him who has no might he increases strength." - Isaiah 40:29

Chapter 12

CPR

"And he said to him, 'Truly, I say to you, today you will be with me in Paradise.'"—**Luke 23:43**

We found a spot— a building where we could host our English classes and mobile clinics in the little village we were serving in. It was an abandoned building in the center of the community. Previously it had been used as a small community center. However, after a young girl committed suicide inside of the building, it had been abandoned. In spite of the building's history, we were willing to make it work. We first had to do a little cleaning and fixing up. The building had become a place for stray dogs to use as a hideout, spiders had taken up every spare corner, and the doors and windows were in complete disrepair.

After we cleaned up the building, it soon became our "home away from home," where we came to serve the people of the community. A church in the States had been following our adventure and sent some funds to provide electricity and a bathroom for the building. And so it began—now people knew where to come, and come they did. English classes were expanded by the three interns that had come to spend a year with us, children's programs were started, and the medical clinic was booming.

One day during clinic, one of the young boys we had gotten to know came running up to the window right beside where I was working with a patient. He was frantic. He could hardly make an intelligent statement come out of his mouth. The only thing I could make out was "VEN! VEN!" *Come!* The wild, panicked look in his eyes spoke the words he couldn't communicate. I grabbed my emergency bag and took off.

I followed him to his house, and there on the couch was his grandfather, in a state of obvious distress. I was able to talk to him for about thirty seconds before he collapsed to the floor, not breathing and with no pulse. The family looked on in horror. I looked down at this eighty-year-old man and knew there was nothing I could do that would change the inevitable outcome, but I did what I could anyway.

I learned early on in my nursing career that much of what you do for a patient is not only for the patient themselves, but for the family members as well. In pediatrics, you don't have just one patient, the whole family is your patient. I've learned to care for the whole family. So this was for them, and not for the dear sweet man lying listless in front of me. I started CPR.

In my mind, I knew two things for certain: this man was not going to make it, and no help was going to come.

In much of the time we lived in Honduras it was the murder capital of the world. There were more murders in this little country than anywhere else in the entire world. And the village we worked in? As bad as the rest of the country. Government officials would not come into the village. The police didn't come. If the electricity went down, the village had to fix it themselves; the electric company wasn't going to come out to fix it. There were no emergency services in town. The fire department was not like the fire department in the United States. There were no trained medical personnel on board. They only put out fires and transported people to the public hospital. There was no public ambulance service; there was only private service. Money was required up front, and they would never come out to the village. The Red Cross was another option, but even they would not come out to this violence-ridden village. You see, this village was run by the local gang, which happened to be MS-13, an international gang known to be one of the most violent gangs in existence. No one else would come; I was the "emergency medical service."

So, I started CPR. Unfortunately, in my career as a nurse, I have done CPR many times. The type of unit I worked on at the hospital ensured this. So I was no stranger to CPR, but this was the first time I had done CPR alone. In a hospital you are surrounded by other medically trained personnel, a crash cart, doctors, respiratory therapists, IV therapists, etc. This time it was just me. My emergency bag contained a CPR mask, an IV start kit, and some epinephrine. So I started CPR…chest compressions, mouth-to-mouth, chest compressions, mouth-to-mouth. I was given a clarity that often happens in times of trial. Some people say that in crisis everything they know goes out the window. God had made my brain a little different— everything streamlines and becomes clear for me. My hand placement, head-tilt/chin-lift, it was all automatic.

It was then that my husband walked into the little house. He had just gone to the airport to pick up our boss who had come from the States to help us with a conference. They both stood there and took in the scene. I needed help. Anyone who has ever done live CPR on a real person, and an adult no less, knows how exhausting it can be. Sure, the adrenaline helps, but let's face it—it's a workout. So I did what we are trained to do, I called out for help—I asked if anyone else knew CPR.

I asked, knowing that my husband knew CPR. We had both been trained and certified as Rescue Divers, and part of this training was CPR certification. Our dive training had been very recent, so I knew my husband knew CPR, but I would NEVER have mandated he help out. So basically, I was giving him an "out."

Helping out in a time of crisis is a messy business. You have to be mentally prepared for any number of possibilities. You have to be emotionally equipped to know that all you give may still not be enough. You have to finish something once you've started. This is not the calling for everyone. I would NEVER call anyone a coward for passing by an emergency situation and not stopping to help. I would NEVER say someone was terrible for not giving CPR to someone if they knew it and did nothing.

Later my sweet husband told me he was going to help out, but for that split second, he didn't know if he could actually do it. But then, he says, he knew that I knew that he knew CPR. He knew what I was asking—he recognized that he was being given an option to "opt out," but he knew that he had to try nonetheless. So he dropped down on his knees next to me and asked how he could help.

I assessed the situation. I had been doing compressions and mouth-to-mouth, and one thing I knew, the mouth-to-mouth was the most difficult in this circumstance. I did have a face shield, but to do mouth-to-mouth on a person who had never had a dental visit in his life, had a mouth full of rotting teeth, and who didn't own a tooth brush—well, I'll leave that to your own fertile imagination what his breath smelled like. As a nurse, I had lived the last twenty years of my life of being vomited on, bled on, pooped upon, peed on, and having various other types of bodily fluids make their way across my path; I once cleaned a young paralyzed girl who was swimming in a pool of feces. I knew my husband had a stomach of steel, but I also knew there were a few things in life that would turn his stomach. So I asked him to do compressions, and I would continue doing mouth-to-mouth.

When our efforts produced no change, I knew I needed to try something else. As my only emergency equipment consisted of my face mask, an IV start kit, and epinephrine, that was my next attempt of rescue. As my husband diligently counted his chest-compressions, I administered epi and tried to start an IV. When I worked at the hospital, I had often been called upon to start IVs on tiny babies down in the ER—the nursing staff in the ER knew that I was a good back-up if they were unable to start an IV. My success rate was very high, but there was no starting an IV on this man.

So, we continued on doing CPR—at least for the family, if not for the sweet man who had died in front of me. After more than thirty minutes of CPR, I gently placed my hands on my husbands' and told him to stop. I "called the code." I looked for a clock to note the time of death and realized there was none to be found, and quite frankly, it didn't really matter. I sat down, placed my hand upon the chest of the man who lay dead before me, and said a prayer. We prayed out loud for this sweet man who had left us this day, and for the family who had been left behind.

In my heart, I knew we had done our best. We had given the family an opportunity to see us try. We had given the family some sort of closure, knowing that they had done what they could do to try and save him. Perhaps it would be enough. We were there when he passed, and he had died surrounded by those who loved him. I lifted my head, to glance around to the twenty or so people who had arrived by that time. In my focus, I hadn't even realized that anyone else was there besides the few of us. I could only hope that they felt we had done what we could. And honestly, we had given this man a chance that almost no one else in this village was given. In this country where the medical system fails its people, where resources are limited, and choices are few, we had given him a chance that most never have.

After praying for the family, we left to give them an opportunity to mourn and grieve their loss. We left to let the community bury one of its own. Not every story has a happy ending. Life on the mission field is full of wonder, full of happy moments, but full of the realities of life as well.

"For by grace you have been saved through faith. And this is not your own doing; it is the gift of God," - Ephesians 2:8

Chapter 13

Levels of Poverty

"A righteous man knows the rights of the poor; a wicked man does not understand such knowledge." – Proverbs 29:7

The day had been exhausting, my mind was done, and my emotions were ragged. I was on my way home from clinic, waiting at one of the few traffic lights in La Ceiba. La Ceiba is a city of 350,000 that amazingly has a Walmart, Burger King, Subway, and even four Pizza Huts. But amidst all of that, the poverty stands out. I looked outside my passenger window and saw a woman about thirty-five or forty years old standing by a small fountain outside of a fairly nice restaurant. It wasn't the fact that she was there that shocked me, it was what she was doing. This woman was gently taking off items of clothing one by one (most likely the only clothes she owned) and carefully scrubbing each piece before putting it back on. She then took a rag, ran it through the fountain, and gave herself a sponge bath. There, in the middle of the city, surrounded by people coming and going in their daily lives. As I slowly drove away with a heavy heart, I wondered who this woman was. What had happened in her life that she found herself alone, washing herself in a public fountain? Never have I been in a place in my life where that was my reality. It left me humbled, and saddened. The image imprinted in my memory, I wanted to hold it dear and not forget it. I prayed that I would always keep that heart for the poor and never forget what I have.

In Honduras, I lived, worked and breathed every day in the midst of poverty. My clinic served the poorest of the poor in the middle of an extremely poor community. I cared for children that had not eaten, who didn't have shoes to wear to school, whose hair was tinged red from being chronically malnourished. Seventy percent of the country of Honduras is considered living in a state of poverty, and the government simply can't support this level of poverty. There simply aren't the resources to provide for the poor. Honduras does not have food stamps, welfare, housing assistance, Obama phones, WIC, health care, free public education, Veterans Hospitals, school lunch program, workers compensation, etc. Street kids are all but absent now, in light of the crack-down on illegal begging. But there is such a thing as legal begging. The disabled and elderly can obtain a certificate with a government seal which permits them to beg on the street.

I lived among this poverty. I worked in this poverty. But I was given the means to live apart from this poverty. I saw children who died of starvation, babies left to die on tables, schools closed because of no funding, hospitals closed because there is no medicine. Even in all that, I was still shocked at times. Because even among the poor there are levels of poverty.

Not long after we arrived in Honduras, we were walking in the downtown area of La Ceiba with our eleven-year-old daughter, Madison. We came across a young street boy curled up in his only t-shirt, sleeping on the street. It was January, and a huge storm had just come through. His clothing was soaked. He was clearly shivering in his wet clothes as he tried to sleep on the sidewalk. I gently leaned over to wake him. He woke with a frightened look on his face—too often street children are beaten, abused, or arrested.

We took him to a used store and bought him a pair of pants and a sweatshirt. I had him go into the little changing room and change out of his wet clothes into the ones we had just purchased. We then walked down the street and bought him lunch. I spent a short amount of time talking to him, but he desperately wanted to leave and take the little food he had left over back to the shack where his sister was waiting. So we prayed for him and sent him on his way.

Madison was so troubled. She said, "Mom, we have SO much, and he has nothing. We need to give everything away and help him."

I told her, "Honey, that is exactly what we have done. And we are here to help people just like him."

I told her not to feel guilty because we had things and he did not. I said it isn't shame on us, it is shame on those that have and do not give as we have been mandated by God to do. If we gave all of what we had to him, how would we help the many others we have come to serve? She gave this some thought and was satisfied.

But there is a cost involved with being a missionary. Being a full-time missionary anywhere is a tough job. Being a full-time missionary in a third world country can be not only physically tiring, but mentally exhausting. My husband was the team leader for Team Honduras and worked forty to sixty hours a week. I was a nurse, had my own clinic, and worked the same forty to sixty hours a week. We didn't work for a paycheck, to make money. I would have stayed as a pediatric nurse manager, and my husband as the second highest paid staffer for the State of California if we wanted to make money. So, it's not about that, but it is about the cost.

Every time a desperate person looks at you with pleading in their eyes and in their voice, and you empty your pockets to find that they are indeed empty and you have nothing financial to give. To look in the face of a person in a medical crisis that only vast amounts of money will fix, and you are not the person that can give it—it costs. And the cost is high.

On a daily basis I am probably asked a minimum of ten to twenty times for something. For food, money, clothing, free medical care, free medicine, free specialty services, free glasses, free something. It is exhausting to be asked day in and day out for things I simply cannot give. The needs of people living in extreme poverty are overwhelming. In Honduras, we ran a high school, a clinic, a street-children program, and a home for single moms. Each had their own challenges, their own needs, but the bottom line was that each of these ministries served people who had nowhere else to turn. To be asked for more than I am already giving—volunteering my time ten or twelve hours a day, always looking for funding to keep my clinic running, food to feed the hungry, clothing to clothe those without, money to pay for things that otherwise wouldn't be paid for—is tiring. To the individual who is asking, it is the most important thing in their life at that time. For me, it is the same story of the ten or twenty people who came before them on that same day.

I have only so much to give—so much money, so much energy, so much food, so much free care, until I have no more to give. I pray that on a daily basis I am filled by Him who CAN give it all—who CAN do all things that I cannot. It reminds me to be reliant on the Master Physician, the Master Farmer, the Master Healer. My real job is to direct others to rely upon HIM and NOT to rely upon me. Because the bottom line is, I can only do what I can do. I can only give what I have, and no more. But there is One who can give all, and in Him I place my trust and reliance. That is when you MUST turn to Jesus. You MUST show that Jesus is the ONLY answer for them.

When you look in your empty pockets or your wallet to find there are no funds, or look in your pantry and there is no food to give, there IS a Source. Jesus tells us in John 4:13-14,

"Everyone who drinks of this water will thirst again; but whoever drinks of the water that I will give him shall never thirst; but the water that I will give him will become in him a well of water springing up to eternal life."

I am broken
I am broken
I am broken for Him

He saw me as I am
And yet He was broken for me

In all my sin
In all my frailties
In all my weakness
He was strong
He lived

He died
He gave it ALL for me

He suffered
He was beaten
He lived for me to be free

He died that I may be free
He lived so I would forever be free
He was the King of Kings
And yet His body broke for me
He was, He is, and He forever shall be
For me...

He is the way
and the truth
and the life

NO one goes to the Father except through Him...

He was pierced
And I was not
He was beaten
I was set free
He was condemned
and I was forgiven

they don't know...
they don't know...
and yet they are forgiven

He is condemned
and we are set free...

The King of Kings

the Lord of Lord
the Bread of Life
The eternal life
The resurrection
The Forever

Christ

"And my God will supply every need of yours according to his riches in glory in Christ Jesus." – Philippians 4:19

Chapter 14

Blue Baby on the Counter

"But Jesus said, 'Let the little children come to me and do not hinder them, for to such belongs the kingdom of heaven.'" – Matthew 19:14

I was a pediatric oncology nurse by trade. I taught childbirth education classes in the U.S. for more than twenty years. What was a tangible way I could help out in a third world country with such limited resources? Well, I could volunteer in the labor and delivery unit at the public hospital. I was a trained nurse, a certified doula and childbirth educator; I thought there was much I could offer.

After going through a convoluted process, I was finally granted access to the labor and delivery floor. The first thing any good nurse does is evaluate her resources and assess the situation. Here is what I saw—an open ward with curtains separating the laboring moms. I was good with this— needing to utilize the limited space, this was the best option. The next thing I immediately saw was the lack of social support for the laboring moms. So I asked around. It was strictly prohibited to have anyone at the bedside beside the laboring mom.

"No one?" I asked.

"No one."

The average first-time pregnancy for a woman in Honduras is fifteen years old. That meant that the majority of these mommies-to-be were teenagers who didn't have an experienced family member to assist them through this process.

The next thing I noticed was that every mommy had an IV. I talked to the nurses there to find out the situation. Here is what I learned: a mother is not admitted to the hospital until she is at least five centimeters dilated. Again, because of the limited space and resources, this was a viable option. Secondly, every woman is started on an IV with Pitocin. Pitocin is used for inducing/ stimulating labor. It is the synthetic version of oxytocin, which is the hormone that our bodies naturally produce during labor. Typically, Pitocin is closely monitored on an IV pump, with very strict rules as to how much and how often it can be increased. At the public hospital there wasn't an IV pump in sight. So the nursing staff did the best they could to figure out the "drip rate" for Pitocin. Drip rate! I had learned this—every nurse does—it's like learning to add before learning to use a calculator. However, ask any nurse working in the United States, and the majority (me included) would not be able to calculate a drip rate without wiping away some serious cobwebs in our memory banks.

But here they were, the nurses in the public hospital, going from bed to bed, using the roller clamp to turn up or down the Pitocin that EVERY mother had running. There was one fetal monitor for the entire ward, so once every two hours the nursing staff would go from laboring mother to laboring mother, hook up the monitor, and evaluate the status of the baby. It was the best they could in the most difficult of circumstances.

The doctors made their rounds as well. At one point, it was decided that one of the mothers needed her bag of waters artificially ruptured. This is a fairly common procedure in the U.S. so I was not surprised by this decision. However, because of the extremely limited resources, lack of linen and pads, the doc ruptured the woman's membranes, assessed the baby, and then went on to examine the next mother. And there the mother sat...and labored...on her bed covered with amniotic fluid. But again—what do you do? You have ONE set of sheets for each laboring woman, you do the best that you can.

I sat with this young woman who was laboring and talked to her. I had been present with many laboring women and had delivered a few babies by myself, so I felt like I could really help this young woman.

We talked about what it was to be a mom—this was her first baby, and her excitement and terror couldn't be veiled. She was scared. She was scared about what she was feeling, the pain she was enduring, and the thought of trying to get through this process by herself. So, we talked about breathing, about controlled pushing, about ways to get through the process. In between contractions I helped her understand what I was looking for—a controlled breathing process through her contraction. We even practiced when she wasn't having a contraction. Then when I felt she was ready, with her next contraction, we did it. However, in the middle of her contraction, she stopped breathing and literally started laughing at my patterned breathing. I knew then this was a lost cause. It actually made me laugh as well. Talk about a foreign concept! There was no such thing as childbirth education classes there. Doulas were something that existed only in other places. So, I stopped breathing with her and was just "with" her. We labored together. I massaged her back and walked her to the bathroom. I was immediately berated for taking the laboring mom to the bathroom, so we went back to the amniotic-soaked bed. It was clear that her time to deliver was imminent. I called the doctor over, and the most amazing thing happened next.

Two things stood out to me. First, they had labor chairs! That was pretty cool! They weren't asking a mother to try and deliver her baby flat on her back. Second, the laboring mother had to crawl to the end of her bed and climb up onto the labor chair. But she made it. The doctor came over, and she pushed. I held her hand and gave her instructions as when to push. The medical staff told her to stop yelling as it "deprived oxygen" from the baby; I whispered in her ear to keep doing what she was doing, because the baby was coming down nicely. The baby's head emerged, but I had some concern. From the amniotic fluid that was coming out, it was clear that there was meconium in the fluid. The baby had experienced some sort of stress and had stooled in utero. The danger with this is that the baby can inhale this stool during delivery, develop pneumonia, and in worst case scenarios, could die.

The doctors tried wiping the baby's mouth and nose, and asked the mom to continue to push. The baby emerged, but if I had to give it an

APGAR score (the score a baby is given that assesses reflexes, color, breathing, etc.) I would have given the baby maybe a two or a three out of ten. The doctor looked at the baby and realized the same thing. The nurse collected the baby, put her on the counter, and returned back to the mom to deliver the placenta.

I looked over at the blue baby on the counter. She was not moving. I couldn't stand there—I had to intervene. I rushed over to the baby, wiped the little nose and mouth and started CPR. I gave tiny little blows into the baby's mouth and nose, and gently pressed the sternum with my thumbs to try and bring the baby to life. The nurses looked over at me and shook their heads. But I couldn't stop.

I continued on this way until some pink showed back in her skin, and her first little cry emerged. She was alive, when only two minutes before she had been lifeless. I found a dirty scrub top (the only thing close by to wrap the baby in) and hugged this little bundle to me, providing what warmth I could. She was moving and breathing. I waited until the doctor and nurses were done with the mom, and she had crawled back into her bed. I walked over to the new mommy and placed the tiny bundle into her waiting arms. She looked at me, and the tears spilled over. She didn't know what had happened. She didn't know that her lifeless baby had been left in the corner to die. All she knew was she had just delivered a sweet little girl into the world.

But then the reality of life in Honduras was presented to me.

A nurse was kind enough to come talk to me after this all had happened. She explained to me why they had done what they had done. There were no ventilators in town, there were no incubators, and IV antibiotics were in short supply. The likelihood that this baby would live through the week was very, very small. They hadn't wanted to give the mother false hope; her baby would probably be dead a week from now. They saw it every day. What I saw as callous nurses and doctors that didn't care was actually just their reality. They knew their limitations. They knew their lack of resources. Only healthy babies survived. I asked her how many babies they lost every week. She instead responded with how many babies they lost EVERY DAY. My heart sank.

I couldn't have changed anything that I did. I wouldn't change anything I had done. But I started to understand what it meant to be a nurse, a medical provider, in a country where resources were so severely limited. A ventilator would cost more than $1200 a day. And that was only if a ventilator was even available. They didn't bother transporting babies to the next big city because they either didn't survive the long trip or they died in the big city hospital because resources there were just as limited. But I still wouldn't change what I had done. I had given that sweet mama and her baby maybe the only few days of life together they would experience. She could carry that with her for the rest of her life. Maybe that would be enough.

Nahum 1:7... The LORD is good, a stronghold in the day of trouble; he knows those who take refuge in him.

For as the heavens are higher than the earth, so are my ways higher than your ways and my thoughts than your thoughts. - Isaiah 55:9b

Chapter 15

The Coup – 2009

"Let every person be subject to the governing authorities. For there is no authority except from God, and those that exist have been instituted by God." – Romans 13:1

The world exploded—at least the world that we knew. The summer of 2009 we were hosting a summer team full of youth. They were staying in our home because we hadn't built our dorm facility yet. Twenty people in total, mostly youth and the couple of adults who had come to be their leaders, when the world started to fall.

We got a premonition of what was happening when the sky started to rain paper. Airplanes flew overhead dropping leaflets upon the crowds of people far below. As the only Spanish speaking people on the team, my husband and I picked up the leaflets, read them, and assured the youth that were in our care that "all was right with the world." In reality, the you-know-what was hitting the fan. The current president wanted to run for reelection. This, however, was strictly forbidden according to the constitution of Honduras. Too many dictators had come into power in Central America, so Honduras had written a constitution prohibiting it from ever happening again. But the current president wanted to run again, so he was going to hold a special election asking the populace if they would agree to another "free election" in which he could run. Even asking was illegal—hence the leaflets that were raining from the sky. The leaflets were clear and simple. They stated that what he was doing was illegal and that everyone should boycott the upcoming election.

Chaos started to rain on the country of Honduras. We shuttled everyone back to our house, and locked the doors up tight—still not giving any light to any of the visiting team about what was happening. But it was inevitable that the word was going to get out, and their families back in the States were going to start to panic.

Here we were, middle-aged Californians, used to stable governments, police forces that worked for the people, and a military that kept the peace; and we found ourselves in the middle of what appeared to be a military coup. What in the world?! The next thing we knew, we were ordered to a complete countrywide lockdown. At 2 a.m. the military arrested the president, in his pajamas, and put him on a plane out of the country. But the plane had nowhere to land. No one would accept this ousted president into their country. Finally, Costa Rica agreed to the landing, and the former president was kicked off the airplane and left in the care of Costa Rica.

Honduras was in turmoil. The senate took over; the Speaker of the House was now President. A curfew was instituted. No one was allowed to leave their house for three days, on penalty of imprisonment. So there we had 20 people in our house, in a state of house arrest. No one could leave. Gratefully we still had internet. We advised everyone to what was happening and gave them all a chance to contact their families back home. We were safe. We had already purchased enough food to last the group's entire trip, so water and food were in sufficient state.

But there we sat…in our house…all twenty-three of us…for three days…

You go on the mission field ready to encounter all sorts of diseases, food intolerances, cultural faux pas, but you never truly embrace what it would look like to live through political upheaval. The United States has obviously seen its fair share of political change, but to most of us, it is a thing of the past. We read about in history books and live it through the experiences of our grandparents. But it is an entirely different thing to experience it live and in person.

We were in a country facing potential political disaster. What did the future hold? The airports were completely closed to incoming and outgoing planes; the military had blocked all exits from the city. We lived on our wits, locked our ten-foot gates, and weathered the tide.

Amazingly enough, the country survived this great upheaval with only a few skirmishes. The new government took over, the system remained intact, and life went on. Once the curfew was lifted, we were able to get the visiting team out on a plane, and we went about our lives, experiencing Honduras as a newly evolving country.

"The Lord is my light and my salvation—whom shall I fear? The Lord is the stronghold of my life— of whom shall I be afraid?" – Psalm 27:1

Chapter 16

Therapeutic Touch

"And Jesus stretched out his hand and touched him, saying, "I will; be clean." And immediately the leprosy left him." –
Luke 5:13

In nursing school we were introduced to the concept of therapeutic touch ("feeling" how a person feels by placing your hands above their body—not touching—and receive their "vibes"). Now, I'm not one to disregard alternative medicine; I definitely think there is a time and place for non-Western medicine.

One thing I DO believe in 100% is physical contact. It is my version of therapeutic touch, if you will. Touching a person acknowledges that you recognize them as a person and communicates that you want to connect with them. I will admit that at times I forget that. In the busyness of seeing many patients and in my desire to reach them all, I am sometimes not as personal as I should be. I like to think that most of the time I genuinely connect with the person in front of me. My time is theirs. I make eye-contact, listen to them, and touch them.

Maria, a sweet seventy-seven-year-old woman came into my clinic. She was suffering from things I simply couldn't help her with. As I reached out to hold her hand, we made eye contact and just connected. One suffering human to another. I was not suffering physically the same way she was, but I suffered from seeing so many suffering. I suffered the pangs of seeing children go hungry, babies born into a difficult world, children neglected and ignored by their parents.

I couldn't identify with Maria's physical suffering, but I could certainly sympathize with it. My sweet mother lived the last ten years of her life with debilitating ailments until she succumbed to the final infection that her poor little body could no longer endure. And in that moment, I saw my mother, suffering things I couldn't even imagine. I couldn't alleviate the physical causes of Maria's suffering, but I loved her with my touch and with my eyes and with my time.

So many of the people we work with are dirty. They are poor; they have only one or two pairs of clothing, lice in their hair, unclipped nails, teeth unclean from never having owned a toothbrush. But what does that matter? Remember the lepers from the Bible—the "untouchables," the "unclean"? And who loved on them? Touch is an essential human connection—it's the reason why being put into prison and isolated from everyone around you is one of the worst forms of punishment. We crave touch, we crave interaction, we crave a community.

Be someone's community. Make eye contact when you talk to someone—and really be engaged. Give them your time. Time is so personal—so intimate, and it's something that you can't get back once you've given it—that's what makes it priceless. So, remember—touch someone. Give them a hug—it may seem like such a small act, but it's one filled with the contact of one human reaching out to another. A sweet friend of mine gave me a mug years ago, because she knew how much I loved her hugs. She just envelops you in them—it's not just a quick squeeze, but one in which I felt wrapped up in the love she wanted to give. The mug says "Free Hugs." And I think of her every time I drink from it. Who have you given a hug to today? Who WILL you give a hug to today?

"Praise be to the God and Father of our Lord Jesus Christ, the Father of compassion and the God of all comfort, who comforts us in all our troubles, so that we can comfort those in any trouble with the comfort we ourselves receive from God. For just as we share abundantly in the sufferings of Christ, so also our comfort abounds through Christ." - 2 Corinthians 1:3-5

Chapter 17

On Being a Nurse

"Is anyone among you sick? Let him call for the elders of the church, and let them pray over him, anointing him with oil in the name of the Lord." – James 5:14

Someone who will cry with you
Someone who will meet your needs before their own are met
Being on time
Going to work even when your own child is sick
meeting people where they are
holding a hand
listening
loving
praying
giving others a chance to be heard
feeling the hurt of others
having other people's bodily fluid on our skin, and not thinking it a
nuisance
being an encourager to someone who has lost the ability to
walk...to speak...to be...
listening to a mother grieve for her child
listening to a child grieve for their lost parent
giving a person a chance to be free from pain
working late to offer one last chance
going to work even when sick knowing others are worse off than
you are
working with shin splints, sore feet, blistered feet

Being honest
a 24-hour job
a job that lives in our blood
until our last breath we still think of ourselves as what our job
depicted us as....

Being a nurse
A gift from God

Chapter 18

A Pig at Clinic

"A righteous man knows the rights of the poor; a wicked man does not understand such knowledge." – Proverbs 29:7

One of the communities where I hosted mobile clinics is a riverside community. We constructed tents with fabric on PVC pipes for privacy screens. Everything could be easily broken down as there is no permanent missionary presence in this village. On one of these clinic days, we had an eighteen-year-old mom come in with her one-year-old son and his sibling. I saw the one-year-old first. The weather had changed here, so tons of kiddos were coming in with "gripe" (a cold). Trying to explain to parents that it was a viral infection, for which there is no magic cure got me a lot of grumpy looks from parents. Unfortunately, many doctors here give in to the requests of patients for antibiotics for viral infections, so when they come to my clinic and don't get any they at times can get very angry. Anyway, this little guy was basically okay.

I took one look at her with her huge belly and red-tinged hair; I couldn't believe she was two-and-a-half. She weighed in at 8.8kg (19.36 pounds). Just to give you an idea, the average two-and-a-half-year-old in the U.S. weighs in at 12.8kg (28.16 pounds), and the WHO (World Health Organization) states that children of her age in Latin America should be about 12.2kg (26.84 pounds). This little one didn't even show up on the chart, she was so underweight. Clearly her eighteen-year-old mother struggled to care for her. This mom was a great candidate for one of our food baskets and our protein-enriched rice.

And finally, at the end of the day, this little guy came to visit us. He was quite cute, but of course, being the nurse—my first thought went to the huge puddles of water around the area we were in (it POURED that day), and the stool that was in the puddles, and the hookworm that comes along with it. This is someone's Christmas dinner.

In eight years of serving in Honduras, I had dogs wander through clinic, chickens clucking at my feet, even a herd of cows brush up against the tent that was my clinic. I've had cats, a toad, and—needless to say—mosquitoes galore, all vying for my attention while I'm trying to see patients. I never thought my "office" would look like this—a tent alongside the river, with dirt for a floor and the wind as my fan. It's a strange and surreal place sometimes. Once in a while I have to step back and look at my life. While I am in the midst of it, it doesn't seem odd, or strange, or different. It's just what I do. But when someone back in the U.S. asks me about my day, or wants additional information, it is then that I reflect on where God has brought me. I am humbled and privileged to be in service to Him.

Chapter 19

Fire

"I came to cast fire on the earth, and would that it were already kindled!" – Luke 12:49

I lifted my head as the very distinctive smell of smoke tickled my nose. Trash is burned quite frequently in Honduras, but my nose knew the difference. This was not trash, and whatever was burning, it was very close. Smoke started to stream into my house through the open windows.

I ran outside and saw the empty field next to our house was on fire. A tree on the property was licked in flame, and dried dead weeds were sprouting spots of new fire. The fire was moving quickly toward our wall. The wall was made of cement, but there were trees growing along both sides of the wall that could easily catch fire and spread it inside of our yard.

I saw one of the neighborhood security guards near the fire, talking on the phone. I could only hope that he was calling the fire department. About fifteen minutes later a fire truck arrived on scene. The firefighters jumped out, armed with a shovel or two, and started spraying water on the big licks of fire running up the tree and the active flames on the outlying bushes. I don't know a lot about putting out a fire of this size, but I know the basics of depriving a fire of oxygen—turning over the embers and digging down to starve the fire. But the shovels remained idle and the water ran out, so they left. There are no fire hydrants in the city and no means of accessing the water mains that run through town. Imagine filling a fire truck with the amount of pressure that comes out of your hose—it would take a day to refill it. So, the firefighters came with only the water that they had in their tank. There would be no refilling of the tank.

As the fire continued to burn, I started making a mental note of what needed to be pulled from the house in case the fire jumped into our yard. I had to decide what was important and what could be replaced. The flames wiped the entire field clean of plants, trees, and all living things. It burned completely up to the wall, and thankfully, there it stopped. You could see the burn marks the next day halfway up the wall. The fire hadn't run out of oxygen; it ran out of fuel. There was nothing left to burn.

As I watched the firefighters, it occurred to me—there was no fire academy here, there was no one to train people here how to put out fires. Without any training, these men did the best that they could, using equipment that was clearly decades old, and it still wasn't enough. What saved the day was that cement doesn't burn. That was the daily reality of life in Honduras.

Considering the very limited resources and the lack of infrastructure in Honduras, I was amazed at what I had taken for granted in the past. I realized that in the States this would have made the news for the terrible job the fire department had done. Communities would have been in an uproar, calling for change, wanting legislation written to prevent anything like this from happening again. Firefighters would have been disciplined, and procedures would have changed.

I think that in the U.S. we have lost touch with what so much of the rest of the world endures on a daily basis. We have no understanding of what it is to live without the conveniences of life, without resources, without an infrastructure that ensures our way of life won't be interrupted by things like a fire. With no property insurance, the house would have been a complete loss, our belongings gone without the ability to replace them. In the U.S. we get irritated when our home owners insurance doesn't send us a check in less than a week after a loss.

I was reading a post on social media not too long ago from someone who was fuming because her doctor had been twenty minutes late! She was angry about having WAITED SO LONG in the air-conditioned waiting room and was texting her frustration from her iPhone 6 on the free wifi to all of her social media accounts. I sat there in wonder. I had just left my clinic in the middle of the jungle where I was caring for a woman whose foot had succumbed to the ravages of uncontrolled diabetes. For over a month I had been trying to save her foot. She hadn't been able to afford the medication that her general practice doctor had told her to take. The endocrinologist that she should have been seeing was so beyond her ability to pay that she had never gone to see him.

This woman came to see me, walking on a foot that constantly oozed puss. She begged and pleaded with me to save her foot; I was just trying to save her life. That day I had to tell her that it was no use—that she was going to lose her foot or the gangrene would take her life.

I went home from the clinic that day and logged onto Facebook to help relieve some of my anxiety from the day when I came across this woman's angry post. She wanted to write a letter of complaint and vowed that she would never be returning to this doctor because she was TWENTY MINUTES LATE. She told all of her friends to never go to this doctor because she couldn't even bother to keep her appointment times. I took a deep breath, and then I kept scrolling—because what I wanted to type in response to her anger would not have been helpful, nor kind. Keeping a grasp on what is important, what is worth fighting for, and what is worth complaining about, is something that each of us should think about before we lose our cool.

"...to one a fragrance from death to death, to the other a fragrance from life to life. Who is sufficient for these things?" - 2 Corinthians 2:16

Chapter 20

Two Teen Girls, Two Pregnancies, Two Different Stories

"And when Elizabeth heard the greeting of Mary, the baby leaped in her womb. And Elizabeth was filled with the Holy Spirit," – Luke 1:41

A young girl of sixteen arrived at the clinic with her sister. She came for a pregnancy test, unsure of the last time she had her period, thinking it was maybe three or four months ago. But she was still totally unconvinced she was pregnant—this was just going to be a test to show she WASN'T pregnant.

"Positivo," I said. Both girls looked at me as if I hadn't said what I just said. "Positive. Pueden ver el resultado." *Positive. You can see the result.*

I showed them the positive exam. There was a long stretch of complete silence. Her sister turned white, which is hard to do if you are Honduran. I was fearful she was going to faint. I looked at the sweet sixteen-year-old in front of me for her response and all I could see was fear, disbelief, and a core-deep sadness. I looked from her back to her sister, who started with silent tears rolling down her face that eventually turned to outright sobs. That is when the pregnant sixteen-year-old started to cry as well.

Now, I have given the diagnosis of a pregnancy to many young women, but never had I received this type of reaction. I asked her sister, "Are you angry? Are you sad? What is going on"

The response I heard tore at my heart. She looked at me with tear-filled eyes and said, "I am terrified."

I looked back at the sixteen-year-old who just nodded her head in agreement. I truly was confused, so I started asking simple questions to try and figure out what her fear was. What I finally learned left me so sad. The man who was the father of this child was truly one of the type you would not want any young girl to be with. I found out that the local gang leader had seen her, and wanted her. He went to her house and told her that she had to come with him or he would hurt her family. As he was a leader of the local MS-13 gang, there was no way she could not go.

The gang leader would NOT be happy with the test results. He had no idea she was at the clinic, nor that she might be pregnant. The situation was horrible, and they truly feared for their family and for themselves. With all that information, we talked for a long time. I prayed with her, and then immediately called my teammate Shannon who had a house for pregnant teenage moms and teenage moms with young children.

A few hours later a young fifteen-year-old girl came into the clinic asking for a pregnancy test. I was not mentally in a good place about the last visitor, so my fears came immediately to the surface. This young girl came with her mother-in-law. The results came back—she was pregnant. I looked from the young fifteen-year-old to her mother-in-law for a reaction. Both of them beamed in excitement; it was clear that this was a happy moment for them.

I sat back, relieved about this particular situation, but still saddened. In the country of Honduras, the average first pregnancy is 15.4 years old! This is in contrast to 24.6 years in the United States. This young fifteen-year-old now was going to be a mommy, and her chances for a future outside of this were all but nill. But I did rejoice that at least this young mom and her future baby were in a "good" situation.

So two young teens, given the same news on the same day, left to two very different situations. Just when I thought I had come to understand life in Honduras, I was faced again with its harsh realities.

"For our citizenship is in heaven, from which also we eagerly wait for a Savior, the Lord Jesus Christ;" – Philippians 3:20

Chapter 21

An Old Pair of Socks

"How beautiful upon the mountains are the feet of him who brings good news, who publishes peace, who brings good news of happiness, who publishes salvation, who says to Zion, 'Your God reigns.'" – Isaiah 52:7

John Bunyan wrote, "You have not lived today until you have done something for someone who can never repay you."

Ruben, a sweet seventy-one-year-old man, came to the clinic with very high blood pressure. This was the first time we had seen him. Our first concern was to take care of his blood pressure, but that soon was followed by caring for his terrible leg ulcer. As he removed his shoes so I could clean his wound, I noticed he had no socks to protect his tender feet from the rubbing of his shoes. I asked him about that, and he responded, "No tengo." *I don't have any.*

I immediately went to my clothing closet and scrounged for some socks. I had no shelves or any other means of putting up the clothes to organize and sort them, so they were still in bags. After looking through all my bags, I couldn't find any socks to give him. I made him promise to return the following day so I could clean his wound again, and I wrote myself a note to bring him some socks from home.

They weren't new socks, but they were good quality with a lot of life left. I brought him three pairs. His face lit up with joy over his "new" socks. I had to give my heart a second to catch up: seeing the joy in his face made it skip a beat. I looked at his feet again and realized that we were in for the long haul. I knew that his hard leather shoes were not going to be conducive to healing.

So once again I went back to my clothing closet to search for a pair of shoes that would work for him. Protruding from the midst of the clothing, the back end of a pair of brown flip flops caught my eye. I knew there was zero chance that these would actually be his size, but I checked them out nonetheless. As I pulled them out, my heart leapt with joy. Sure enough, these would fit my sweet patient.

With a pair of socks and the flip flops in tow, I went back to him. I cleaned and dressed his wound, and covered his feet with the new-to-him socks. His face lit up. With tears streaming down his face, he thanked me for the first pair of "new" socks he had had in ten years. Then I fitted his feet in the flip flops (yes, over his socks), so his shoes wouldn't rub on his wound. He looked at me like I was a saint. I looked at him and my heart leaped with joy! How many pairs of socks had I thrown out in my lifetime? How many pairs of shoes had gone to the trash instead of to Goodwill? This simple act had absolutely changed this man's life.

In Ruben's continuing care, it was clear that he had been unable to wash his foot or trim his nails for a long time. It is times like this when being a nurse isn't about delivering medicine, drawing blood, or giving instructions. It is times like this when it is about connecting with someone, offering the gift of touch, or simply washing someone's foot that hasn't been washed in months. To trim nails and to give care that is not necessarily about physical care, but emotional and spiritual care—it is times like this that I am privileged to be a nurse. Over the next month Ruben visited our clinic every day, and I cleaned and dressed his wound until it was completely healed. His leg was saved. His life was changed. My life was changed—with the simple act of offering a pair of socks.

"[34]Then the King will say to those on his right, 'Come, you who are blessed by my Father; take your inheritance, the kingdom prepared for you since the creation of the world. [35]For I was hungry and you gave me something to eat, I was thirsty and you gave me something to drink, I was a

stranger and you invited me in, [36]I needed clothes and you clothed me, I was sick and you looked after me, I was in prison and you came to visit me.' [37]"Then the righteous will answer him, 'Lord, when did we see you hungry and feed you, or thirsty and give you something to drink? [38]When did we see you a stranger and invite you in, or needing clothes and clothe you? [39]When did we see you sick or in prison and go to visit you?' [40]"The King will reply, 'Truly I tell you, whatever you did for one of the least of these brothers and sisters of mine, you did for me.' Matthew 25:34-40

[10]Jesus answered, "Those who have had a bath need only to wash their feet; their whole body is clean. And you are clean, though not every one of you." [11]For he knew who was going to betray him, and that was why he said not every one was clean. [12]When he had finished washing their feet, he put on his clothes and returned to his place. "Do you understand what I have done for you?" he asked them. [13]"You call me 'Teacher' and 'Lord,' and rightly so, for that is what I am. [14]Now that I, your Lord and Teacher, have washed your feet, you also should wash one another's feet. [15]I have set you an example that you should do as I have done for you. [16]Very truly I tell you, no servant is greater than his master, nor is a messenger greater than the one who sent him. [17]Now that you know these things, you will be blessed if you do them. John 13:10-17

Chapter 22

Gangs, Guns, and God

"The Lord tests the righteous, but his soul hates the wicked and the one who loves violence." – Psalm 11:5

A new gang moved into our community of Armenia Bonito. They were associated with the notorious international MS-13 gang. In their first few weeks in the community the number of murders increased. The community was frightened. Some families kept their kids inside and avoided the streets.

Mike and Jesús, the pastor of our new church plant, felt it was important to open a dialogue with the gang, so they went looking for the gang's leader. They asked the other gang members where they could find the leader. Word got out and this spooked the gang. One day two gang members approached our truck with guns pointed at Mike and Jesús. They flung the doors open, dragged Mike and Jesús out of the truck, and shoved them to the ground. After searching the car for guns they kicked Mike and Jesús repeatedly and put guns to their heads.

"Why are you here? What do you want?" the young men screamed as they pressed the guns tighter to their heads.

With hands raised, Mike replied calmly, "Relax, we are not here to bother you. We only want to introduce ourselves and talk to you."

"Who are you?" the gun-wielding men asked.

Standing up, Mike said, "This is Pastor Jesús. He is the pastor of the new church, and I am Mike. I am the missionary who owns the new medical clinic."

Relaxing a bit, the gang members put away their guns, lit up a few joints to calm down, and apologized, "We're sorry we hurt you, but we are here to protect this community and we didn't know why you were looking for us."

Jesús reassured them that they understood, and Mike asked if they could buy the men a soda and sit down together to talk. Within minutes Mike and Jesús were surrounded by a dozen soda-drinking gang members. During their 30-minute conversation, Mike refused to pay a "protection" fee, but offered free medical care to any of the guys at our clinic. Everyone was content as they parted ways.

A week later Umberto, one of the gang's members, approached Jesús and said he wanted to talk. Over the course of a week Mike and Jesús talked with him several times. They gave him a Bible and talked about Christianity. Umberto became a Christian, but he was scared. He wasn't sure if the gang would let him leave.

Mike and Jesús agreed to meet with Umberto and the gang to ask if he could leave. They brought plenty of Bibles and gave one to each member of the gang. After Umberto announced to his fellow gang members that he was a Christian, Jesús asked the gang leader if Umberto had his permission to leave the gang. The leader looked at all the members and said, "If any of you want to leave the gang because you want to follow God, you have my permission." Two more gang members later approached Jesús, became believers and left the gang. We pray that God will continue to impact the hearts of these young men.

Chapter 23

Frustration

"Do not neglect to do good and to share what you have, for such sacrifices are pleasing to God." – Hebrews 13:16

People disappoint... government disappoints... circumstances disappoint. Why does this surprise me every time it happens?! I always hope and pray for the best, get excited about opportunities, want everything to be "perfect" in the end, and when none of the above happens I'm crushed! My sweet husband has had to tell me over and over to guard my heart because guess what? People WILL disappoint...government WILL disappoint...circumstances WILL disappoint.

We had a sweet elderly gentleman come into the clinic with multiple complaints, but his primary complaint was stomach pain. Our doctor started with an abdominal exam—only to find this:

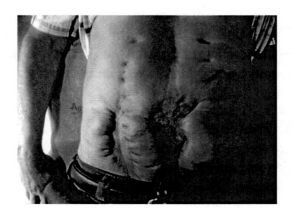

It was an old bullet wound gone wrong. Nine surgeries later, this is what this gentleman had to live with. Botched work, bad surgery, no skin grafts, and a mound of infections. He had so much scar tissue internally that it was most likely adhering to his intestines and causing his severe stomach pain. All we could do was to treat the symptoms, nothing more, and pray with him and for him.

Another big frustration was a young—VERY young—new mother with a three-week-old infant. She had not given her baby the medication prescribed to her earlier in the week, and the baby was now so sick that our doctor advised immediate hospitalization. However, the young mother was more interested in the visit of the baby's father than in caring for her child. Over an hour and a half after our clinic was closed, we were still trying to convince her of the gravity of her situation and the seriousness of her child's illness. Babies that sick in the States are oftentimes in the ICU and sometimes even on a ventilator. If this moter didn't make the right decision, and soon, it would be too late for her baby.

I do not know what the outcome of that situation was, but I felt a sense of helplessness. There is no means of intubation at the public hospital, and her baby could have died. There are levels of frustration that just tear at the heart of what it is to be a pediatric nurse. I realize that things won't always work out right or even the way I want them to. I need to rest in the fact that we do the best we can, give the best medicine we can, share the best education with our patients that we can, but that ultimately most of what we do is out of our hands. I could only pray that mom made the right decision before it was too late.

> *"Only give heed to yourself and keep your soul diligently, so that you do not forget the things which your eyes have seen and they do not depart from your heart all the days of your life; but make them known to your sons and your grandsons." – Deuteronomy 4:9*

Chapter 24

A Mother to Many

"Honor your father and mother, and, you shall love your neighbor as yourself." – Matthew 19:19

When you live in a country where the average first time pregnancy is at fifteen years old, the family size is quite large. It is not unheard of to have anywhere from four to eight children in any household. More often than not, the nine-year-old is held responsible for caring for the babies in the house while the mother takes care of household chores. Living in a community like Armenia Bonito means handwashing your clothing and collecting firewood to start the fire to cook your food. It means caring for your children, feeding them, and getting them to school. It is hard work.

I started a Kids Club because I wanted a place for young children to be able to be a part of something bigger than themselves and to learn about God. The program quickly grew to over 100 children. I taught them the books of the Bible and the Children's Catechism, provided them with small meals, helped them with crafts, and always had fun games to play. I gave them a place to belong and just be a kid! They loved the opportunity to set aside adult responsibilities for a little while. Because I was able to be there for kids, take care of their boo-boos, and give them hugs and kisses, I became the mother that many didn't have.

One day we got a phone call from our teammates just before they were to leave on furlough. They wanted to meet with us. A year earlier they had taken into their home an 18-month-old Honduran boy. His mother had been a resident at our home for single teenage moms and their babies. She ended up having to be removed because of a mental illness we simply weren't prepared to deal with, but she had this sweet little eighteen-month-old. We couldn't turn him out on the streets. So our teammates took in this little guy and raised him with their four older children.

Now that they were headed back to the States on furlough, our teammates had a problem. The U.S. Embassy would not give him permission to enter the U.S. because he was Honduran and his mother was still living. They had nowhere for this little guy to stay while they were out of the country. So they asked us. Here we were, two middle-aged people, with a teenage daughter, being asked to bring a now two-and-a-half-year-old into our house. Wow! But how could we say no? Otherwise this little guy had nowhere to go. So, we agreed.

We had been parents to our own daughter, and I had been a "mother" to so many children in the village where we worked, but now we were full-time parents to a toddler. He came to us still in diapers, in a crib, and still drinking from a sippy cup. Summer teams had arrived, and we were neck deep in organizing and hosting summer teams, with a child of our own, and now a toddler. So in the midst of running a full-time clinic, hosting and running summer teams, and caring for my daughter, I set out to train up this little Honduran boy.

In the six months we had him, we potty trained him, took him out of a crib, had him drinking from a normal cup, and even started teaching him his ABCs. We had the privilege of reading books to him every night and praying with him in Spanish. We loved this little boy fiercely—we celebrated his third birthday, bought him presents for Christmas, and Madison was a big sister to him. We incorporated him into our family, but we knew that our time with him would end.

When our teammates returned from furlough after six months, there certainly was a time of mourning. We gave back this little guy who had become so much a part of our lives. It is likely he will not remember his time with us, as long-term memories don't really form until about age four, but what will stick with him is that he was loved and cherished for the time he was with us—he had a sense of belonging and family that he wouldn't have otherwise had.

"The Christian who is pure and without fault, from God the Father's point of view, is the one who takes care of orphans and widows, and who remains true to the Lord--not soiled and dirtied by his contacts with the world." – James 1:27

Chapter 25

I am my Own Doctor

"And he said to them, "Doubtless you will quote to me this proverb, 'Physician, heal yourself.' What we have heard you did at Capernaum, do here in your hometown as well.'" - Luke 4:23

Since becoming a missionary nurse I've had the opportunity to do all sorts of "fun" things. Lanced many an abscess, packed wounds, given stitches, started IVs on the field, delivered babies—that kind of thing. However, it has always been on someone else!

I am not one of those "do unto others, but not unto myself" kind of people. I actually really enjoy doing procedures. Whenever we had a procedure at clinic that needed to be done, my doctor always called me in to do it. Start an IV, draw some labs, remove a toenail, do some stitches—I'm your girl! It's that feeling of having accomplished something that others either wouldn't or couldn't do. It was a feeling of satisfaction in a job well done.

I got a chance to do a little self-treatment after running my first marathon. We were on furlough, and I knew this would be my only chance to actually run one. So we trained for it, and a week prior to returning to Honduras, I ran the marathon. Mike promised me that losing toenails is something that many runners experience. Well, after over 600 miles of training and then running the marathon, I noticed that my big toe started to turn green underneath the nail. Then I noticed that toenail next to it was almost completely detached.

It took me few hours to get up the courage to go upstairs and prepare what I needed for my minor surgery. I pulled out the lidocaine, scrubbed my foot with iodine, donned my gloves, pulled out a syringe and injected a 1½ inch needle between my toes to give myself a digital block. I didn't want to feel this after all. Once I felt the lidocaine had been given sufficient time to take effect, I then proceeded to shove a hemostat underneath the toenail to separate it from the skin underneath. Basically, you separate the nail from the nail bed (think wartime torture methods). Yeah…that's what I was doing to MYSELF! I could feel the nail separating from the nail bed as I worked the hemostat further and further down. As soon as they were two separate entities, I grabbed the nail with the hemostats, rolled it sideways, and completely removed it from the nail bed. Yes...all by myself...alone…upstairs on my floor...and I didn't pass out in the process. I must admit, there WAS a small moment where my stomach turned over, but I knew that I didn't have a back up—that I had started this and had to follow it through to the end.

Another day… another situation…

I started getting sick on a Sunday night. I had serious chills, a 102° fever, and aches all over my body. I was wiped out and generally feeling like crap. As it was 10 o'clock at night, I took some acetaminophen and ibuprofen and went to bed, sweating and shaking for the rest of the night. The following day I found pus and blood in my urine. *Hmmm... I thought. This is pretty serious. Probably should start some meds.*

So I started some oral meds (quite appropriate for a general run-of-the-mill urinary tract infection, but not really so much for a full-blown kidney infection). But I'll be honest, I was a little delirious. I thought I was making some fairly rational decisions, even though I couldn't shake the super high fever and chills. I had Mike run to the store and get me some injectable meds and had Madison give me the injection. She had done this before when I had a pretty bad staph infection, so with a quick reminder of how to do it, she gave me the shot.

Even with the injection I was still suffering from high fever and chills. My husband was endlessly asking if I should go be seen. That was when my BFF, Mindy, stepped in and gave me quite a tongue lashing (at least the best you can do) over Facebook chat. Then came the phone call and the brow beating.

"I don't want to lose you," she said, "You could go septic and I could lose you."

That did get my head cleared a bit and got me thinking. But I can surely take care of myself, right? I'm pretty smart, drinking lots of fluids, taking my little meds...surely I can take care of this...can't I?

I know—any rational person at this point would have realized the error of their ways and called it quits. But if you know me well enough, you know I am NOT a quitter! And I'm stubborn. And I think I know best.

Yes, that was the way my brain was working. By admitting defeat, I was admitting I couldn't do it myself. And this is where my sin becomes glaringly obvious to everyone else, but I still couldn't see it. But Mindy, who is also a nurse, was not giving up without a fight. We started the compromise game.

"If you aren't better in 30 minutes after your meds you are GOING IN," she said.

"What?" I replied, "That's not even time for it to start working! How about 10 p.m. tonight?"

"Oh, HECK no!" she said. "How about in four hours?"

We reached a final compromise that if I still was sick the next day I had to PROMISE to go and be seen, or there would be phone calls made.

That promise made me go. Even after another terrible night, I was trying to convince myself that I really didn't need to go. But because of the promise I made and the value I place on holding true to my word (and knowing how much my BFF loves me), I went.

Thankfully I had an amazing clinic with an incredible doctor and an amazing nurse who, upon taking the first look at me, had an IV with two liters of fluids up and a massive dose of antibiotics running before I even realized it. I still had a very high fever and was a bit delirious, crying and feeling awful. But they weren't messing around.

As I sat there on the exam bed, sweating through my fever in the jungles of Honduras in a clinic that God had built, I began to see the last couple of days in a different light. What an idiot I was. What indeed could have happened? A friend of a friend had just died of the same thing I had—because she hadn't gotten medical attention in time. Obviously, my paltry means of trying to take care of things probably held off what could have ended very badly.

I was reminded of time after time my husband asking if I should go to be seen—was I SURE I was okay? Of my friend's relentless pursuit of me—and I knew that once again God had brought me low only to lift me up by showing me His love through His people. From my family taking care of me, to my friend's loving berating; from my doc's simple hug and pat on my head as I cried into his scrub top because I was so exhausted and so, so sick, to sweet nurse Angy's compassionate caring for me while at the clinic.

Pride—my biggest sin—showed itself again, and once again, God was sanctifying me through the process. I firmly believe that you could pretty much look at every sin committed and trace it down at its base to originate from pride. When you think your decisions have to make more sense than what God tells you is best for yourself. Isn't that pride? In our sinful nature we don't want others telling us what to do. Look at that stubborn toddler and that willful teenager. They certainly feel like their decisions are the right ones and ours are not. We, in the eyes of God, have to be those stubborn toddlers and willful teenagers, right?

I know He looks down at us every time we turn from his direction and says, "Silly child! But I still love you—looks like I need to teach you this lesson again."

This was a life lesson. Batted down once again by a God who loves me so much and wants me to listen. Just listen. Don't speak...just listen. The word listen is a verb, which implies that it is an action. I need to actively be involved in the process.

"Soar back through all your own experiences. Think of how the Lord has led you in the wilderness and has fed and clothed you every day. How God has borne with your ill manners, and put up with all your murmurings and all your longings after the 'sensual pleasures of

Egypt!' Think of how the Lord's grace has been sufficient for you in all your troubles." - Charles H. Spurgeon

Chapter 26

The Missionary Mother of a Teenage Kid

"Train up a child in the way he should go; even when he is old he will not depart from it." – Proverbs 22:6

Our team was full of moms. But our different stages in life and our different approaches to the mission field left us worlds apart. All of the other moms on our team had little ones, so the majority of their time was spent at home caring for them. But I was different. Before we came to the mission field, I had lived a life in the middle: working full-time and homeschooling full-time. It was the best of both worlds, but it was a choice that wasn't understood by either the stay-at-home moms or the working moms around me. It was no different with our team. But that was okay—because I was determined to be the best full-time mom, full-time wife, and full-time missionary I could be.

The other moms on the team excelled at being stay-at-home moms, but I wanted the best of both worlds and I was determined to get it. I was able to get my girl to school each day, spend the entire day working and doing ministry, then pick her up after school and help her with her homework and school activities, make dinner, and be a wife. It was great...but I was alone in it. I was surrounded by a multitude of people, but I was alone. No one, besides my husband, "got" me. The other moms on the field didn't know what it was like to live both lives, so even though I was surrounded by a team full of moms, I was alone.

Another odd place to be was as an older mom of an older child on the mission field. You can go online and find any number of blogs, advice columns, and support groups for the new mom with the new baby on the mission field, but almost NO support for the older mom with the older child. Often people don't think about the life of a mother of a teen on the mission field. Mostly, people think of the young mother with young children. Not often does one think of the older mom. What does it mean to have a teenager on the mission field?

My young girl – becoming a woman
Have I raised her in a godly manner?
Have I given her the ability to resist temptations?
When I am not with her, does she look to her God?

When troubles arise
in a school she does not know
in a culture she does not know
with peers she can't relate to
what will happen?

When she comes home crying
because she can't speak the language
When she struggles in class
when classmates make fun of her
How do I respond?

When she struggles through hormones
When she realizes that her clothes matter
when her hair matters
when her looks matter
She still comes to me and is looking just for a hug.

The mother of a teen on the mission field
Who struggles with her own inadequacies
But not letting those show to her daughter

Who is trying to deal with her own.

The mother of a teen trying to model a godly woman
trying to BE a good woman
trying to be a wife and a mother
But struggling with all the responsibilities of ministry work.

Where is the balance?
No one sees the struggles
No one sees the pleading with God to ease the pain of her child
No one sees the tears as her child relays the pains she is going
through.

The hours of homework help
The books you read to help you understand
The hours on your knees for your child
The lectures
The mother/ daughter talks
The laughter, The crying together
Knowing there will be things she will miss
No prom to attend
No dances at all
No clubs to be involved in.

But the joy she is receiving in the experiences she has
That's she's NOT a missionary kid, but a kid missionary
That she is learning another language
That she thrives in caring for others outside of herself
That she loves on kids in the village
That she is just herself.

So as I realize there are so few who understand my situation
that there are few who relate or even think of my struggles
I stand in the knowledge that my God cares for my child
that He gives her just what she needs

And gives me just what I need.

I have a missionary kid (MK), or as my daughter fondly calls it, a "kid missionary." She has been out of her birth country for the majority of her growing-up years, including the junior high and high school years. I have been around a lot of MKs, and I wonder if we treat them right. Do we allow them to be their own person, or do we mold them to what we want them to be? These kiddos don't really have a place they call "home." Home is where they are currently living. If you ask an MK where they are from, you will get a quizzical look with varied responses. Is where they are from where they were born? Where they went to school? Where they currently are?

In the U.S., when a child that has one or more parent from a country outside of the U.S., we encourage that child to understand their ancestral roots. We encourage them to celebrate activities, events, and holidays from both their home country and the country of their roots. We encourage language acquisition of both their home country and their country of origin. I wonder then why we give that all up when we go on the mission field. Why do we get so single-minded in becoming entrenched in our new host country that we abandon where we came from?

Since I have been on the mission field, I have traveled all over the world and met MKs in places all over. We have had regional retreats with missionaries and families from all over Latin America, and I have talked with many an MK. Just recently I spent some time with an MK getting ready to go back to the States, and I asked her what she was going to do after college. "I will never stay in the U.S. after I graduate," was her response. I wondered since when did it become the norm to instill disdain for the U.S. in our MKs?

I did a quick, unofficial survey of MKs and found that many don't know the National Anthem, the Pledge of Allegiance, the U.S. capitol, the name of the Vice President, or why we celebrate on the 4th of July. How many MKs know why we have stripes on the flag? What is their significance? Who is known for having crafted the flag, and who were the founding fathers?

We need to lift up our MKs—to love them for the unique people they are and to encourage them that it's okay to be different, to not know how to answer the question "Where are you from?" But also to recognize the unique things that make them who they are, to allow them to embrace ALL the countries they are from, to share their history with them.

When we dropped Madison off at college, the first few days of orientation were just for the international and missionary kids. When all was said and done, the announcer said to the kids, "Now take care, because tomorrow the Americans arrive." It was funny and we all laughed, because we acknowledge the uniqueness that our kids are— that Third Culture Kid—not a kid of one country or another, but unique in their own culture.

I wrote some cards for my girl before she headed off to college— thirty in all. Some advice that seemed suited for what she would experience and for what was ahead of her. I sealed each one up and put dates on the envelopes for her to open one each day. Here are a few of them:

1. When you were two years old, "NO!" was not an acceptable answer to what I asked of you. However, "No" is now not only an acceptable answer, but given certain circumstances, the best response of all.

2. Share what you have. If you have two coats, give one to another.

3. It is always better to give than to receive, but never at another's expense. If it is a blessing to someone else to give to you, accept with a humble heart.

4. The world is going to try and get you down, but you must remember, "You're braver than you believe, and stronger than you seem, and smarter than you think." – Christopher Robin to Winnie the Pooh, from "Pooh's Grand Adventure: The Search for Christopher Robin."

5. The needs of the many outweigh the needs of the few...or the one... - Spock

6. The needs of the one are sacrificed for by The One - God

7. I love you for your uniqueness. Some others won't appreciate it, but "The things that make me different are the things that make me." - Piglet, A.A. Milne – Winnie-the-Pooh

8. And remember—in "true" vampire lore, vampires NEVER say, "MUAH!"

9. One never gets lost: you are only on an adventure. And MAN did we have MANY an adventure.

10. Man looks on the outside, but God looks at the heart. You are not only beautiful on the outside, but on the inside too. God must smile when he looks at you.

11. Your faith is your own, not your parents'. "Train up a child in the way he should go; even when he is old he will not depart from it." Proverbs 22:6

12. When you eventually look for the man who will be your future husband, use your father as a guide. Look at the way he treats me and loves me. I know those are high standards to hold to, but you deserve no less.

13. I am your mother first and always, and although you are an incredible young woman, a part of me will always hold you in my heart as my baby. "I'll love you forever, I'll love you for always...as long as I'm living my baby you'll be." - Love you Forever by Robert N. Munsch

Chapter 27

Oh, Wow. Where's Honduras?
(written by Madison Pettengill from Africa, at twenty years old)

Traveling is fun. Going somewhere new, even if it's for work or missions, is novel and engaging. You walk the streets as an outsider, looking to enjoy the newness of a place that is strange to you. It is weird, foreign—it may seem backwards. You smile at the buildings around you, at how different they are. You pause, half afraid, as you are handed local food. Wait, what is this? People actually eat this?

Traveling is strange, educational, an adventure. Most importantly, though, it's temporary. You have fun, you work hard, and you may touch hundreds of lives, but you're not there to stay. At the end of your trip, you pack up and leave. Exposing yourself to such strange new cultures is exhausting. Now it's time to go back home where it's safe. Back to the weirdness you know. Back to the idiosyncrasies you understand. Where you can find canned bok choy sitting snugly next to a package of taco shells. Where a forty-foot Old Glory flies proudly over every car dealership.

But where does that leave me? Lost and confused in the sea of a culture I don't understand? Sometimes. I'm twenty years old now. I'm a graphic design major in my sophomore year. My peers are well-meaning college kids who've never owned a passport. Many have no possible frame of reference for the kind of poverty I've seen. My classmates sit in the cafeteria debating about Bernie Sanders or how to fix the college tuition bubble, while I look on in honest confusion.

During a group project, it's only a matter of time before someone makes a pop culture joke I don't understand. Then someone will ask me why I didn't get it, and we've all tipped down the rabbit hole. I sigh and decide how much I want to say. The same quick calculations flick through my brain: How much geography am I willing to explain? What's my audience—am I going to have to sugarcoat things or can I speak my mind? Will this conversation derail our project efforts? Do I think they actually care?

I can tell the people around me what I've gone through, if I want. When they ask, I'll mechanically list off the same answers to the same questions that these same kinds of people have asked me a thousand times. I can deflect with humor, pretending to be the quirky little foreigner who just didn't get it. Or I can be blunt. I didn't understand your joke because I have spent eight years living in the country with the highest murder rate in the world. I knew a three-year-old who starved to death. My high school's armed guard was stabbed in the back of the neck with a machete during his night shift. My third option, however, is deciding not to be a jerk.

It's frustrating, sometimes, when people don't understand. Now and again it's tempting to get angry at the people who don't care. When the forty-year-old lady in front of me seems personally offended that the bedraggled Subway worker can't give her a vegan Meatball Marinara (true story), I get upset. But I learned long ago that yelling at people earns me nothing but high blood pressure and a foul mood. The job of a missionary is to meet people where they are. If I can do that when I am in Honduras, why can't I do the same when I am in America?

Perhaps for me, American culture is a special kind of weird. I was born in California. Long before we became missionaries, the Pettengills had two cars, two motorcycles, a pool, a nice house, and an annual pass to Disneyland. My life was nothing but privilege for twelve years. I did not know hunger, loss, dirtiness, fear, or death. I could not possibly understand poverty. How could have I imagined a place like Honduras, where families had to choose between starving to death and abandoning one of their children? But when I moved to Honduras it became my reality.

I soon came to see Honduras as home. I went to middle school and had problems. I went to high school and had slightly fewer problems. My best friends stopped speaking to each other. Our house was broken into. The president was forcibly ousted. My grandmother died. All of these powerful, personality-shaping events happened to me in Honduras. Honduras is where I grew as a person, where I fought through some of my hardest moments. It was the place I associated with personal strength and emotional growth. For me, the U.S. is a symbol of nostalgia. It is my childhood when things were fun and simple and easy. Honduras, then, is a symbol of me as a person. It's the place where I really developed into who I am now. So I see the conveniences of the U.S., and I have memories of when life was that easy. But now, it's frustrating when people view those conveniences as a birthright.

Some may read my words and feel worried or angry. Clearly this missionary kid hates America. She resents her past, or maybe her nostalgia does not live up to reality. She's a foreigner with a U.S. passport. Nothing could be farther from the truth. It's easy to critique something from the outside. Because I've lived outside of Western culture for so long, it's easy to see the flaws. I shake my head in bemused confusion at 7-11's Big Gulps. I smile, a little overwhelmed when I see the U.S. flag is displayed on every available surface. I stand in awe at the genius behind Red Box, and then wonder why I'm the only one who sees it.

But now I am the traveler. I go to Seattle and smile at the strangeness of the buildings. I go to Atlanta and pause, half afraid, at the grits handed to me. I've experienced things that many of my peers cannot understand, and it has shaped me to become the person I am now. My adolescence may have looked much different from yours, but I will never be ashamed of being a Kid Missionary.

"Behold, children are a gift of the LORD, The fruit of the womb is a reward. Like arrows in the hand of a warrior, So are the children of one's youth. How blessed is the man whose quiver is full of them; They will not be ashamed When they speak with their enemies in the gate."-Psalm 127:3-5

Chapter 28

Haiti

"Not that we are sufficient in ourselves to claim anything as coming from us, but our sufficiency is from God, who has made us sufficient to be ministers of a new covenant, not of the letter but of the Spirit. For the letter kills, but the Spirit gives life." – 2 Corinthians 3:5-6

January 29th, 2010. I stepped onto the devastated streets of Haiti. "The" earthquake had happened—devastation hit. In a few short minutes, the lives of 250,000 people had been cut short. More people had lost their lives in one city than were lost in all the countries affected by the 2004 tsunami.

Part of my DNA is to help people. I have an ever-driving need to do it. I can't look away. A car accident on the side of the road, a sorrowful person at our clinic—whatever the need, my DNA reaches out to that person that I am compelled to help.

So there I was, driving through what looked like the war-torn streets of Haiti, wondering what in the world would I do. The smell of rotting corpses enveloped us as we drove down streets where bodies were still buried underneath rubble and probably would forever stay. I held my breath not to take it in, as my brain denied the reality of what my senses were telling me. I tried not to think about the families that were lost, that would not be remembered. How could I possibly be a part of this story? How could I help? This is not a story of heroics, not a story of pulling people from rubble or coming to the rescue of someone on the brink of death (although there was plenty of that); this is the story of just being available. I am the pinky finger on the great hand that serves our God. I go where He calls and serve how He calls me to serve.

The first week or so our Disaster Relief team served a refugee camp in Port-au-Prince. We brought healing both physically and mentally to people who were living in tents and trying to scrape by with what little they could scavenge. I lived off of rice alone and lost ten pounds. I showered in my clothing under a hose and "washed" my clothes at the same time. One set of clothes to wear, and one set of clothes to change into. I changed in my sleeping bag and hung out my wet clothes to dry for the next day. I awoke bleary-eyed after trying to sleep with the constant drone of a military generator. The latrine system left much to be desired and potable water almost nonexistent, but our team persevered.

Then the administrator of a local "hospital" came to us and asked if we would consider helping them. There was a hospital that had been abandoned since the '70s that the French had taken over during this crisis. The need there was overwhelming. In the hospital itself there were more than 150 ICU patients lying on mats, cardboard boxes, or whatever could be found. Four times as many patients were living in makeshift tents on the perimeter of the hospital.

So for the next two and a half weeks we endeavored to make a difference in this place. Our team of MTW folks worked the night shift—a grueling 16 hours at a time. It was rough! Our little team was managing the 150 ICU patients lying on the floor with whatever medical equipment we could scrounge up.

During change of shift one day, all the doctors and nurses went to the front of the hospital to give report about what had transpired in the last 16 hours of the night. I looked around and realized that the 150 patients were going to be left unattended, so I made the decision to stay on duty. Just then, in walked a pregnant woman in ACTIVE labor, and there I was—by myself.

She was breathing heavily, an obvious sign of advanced labor. I looked frantically around me—there was no one there who could translate for me, and the only thing I could think was "No." No...not here...no, not now...no, not by myself...no, not in this grime and despair…no, not on the filthy floors of this once-abandoned hospital. But as she looked at me, without a common tongue, the language of "mom" spoke volumes! The baby was coming—there was no "No"—it was time.

I frantically looked around me. There were no other medical people in sight, but in a desperate plea to appease my own sanity, I yelled out, "WE ARE HAVING A BABY HERE!"

But no one heard; no one came running. I grabbed this mom's hand and took her outside our hospital and found the leftover cardboard box "bed" of someone we had lost the night before, and I laid her down there. She was alone…I was alone…and the look in her eyes was one of complete terror.

I taught childbirth education for over twenty years before I left for the mission field. I did an internship for over a year in a maternity ward, delivering many babies. But then I had resources—other nurses, doctors, an OR that could save her from the potential complications of childbirth, monitors that would tell me the baby's heartbeat and contractions. I panicked. I was completely alone, with no one around, I didn't even speak her language, and a pregnant mom was looking to me for answers—looking at me to make things right. I kept thinking, *I'M JUST A NURSE!... WHAT DO I KNOW?* But God knew, and He would equip me and give me just what I needed.

I steadied my breath, prayed a very serious, very quick prayer to the One who knows all—for wisdom beyond my own, and to the Physician of all—to grant me the ability to make this happen. I met this mom's eyes, and in the unspoken words of someone who was here to help, I communicated that I was here for her. I would make it all right.

Like any good soldier, like any good nurse, like any good Christian, I dug down deep. *What do I know? What are my resources? What do I have available to me?* I had two alcohol swabs, one pair of clamps, one pair of bandage scissors, and God. Those were my resources, and that was sufficient. I laid this sweet mama down and donned my one pair of gloves. I was ready to give this soon-to-be mama my best.

I pried her legs apart to confirm that the baby was clearly coming. That was all it took—she bore down and her bag of waters broke, spraying me with amniotic fluid. The baby's head was already presenting. I checked for the umbilical cord, which was wrapped around the baby's neck. I gently removed it. Without any type of suction, I wiped the baby's nose and mouth clear of amniotic fluid, and in English I encouraged the mama to push. It didn't matter that we didn't speak the same language, it was clear what needed to be done.

The mama pushed and pushed again, and out came a beautiful little girl. I looked in complete amazement as this precious life, in the midst of all this death and destruction. I cried, incredulous to the miracle I was seeing before me. Amidst the anguish and peril of what I had been seeing and witnessing and the patients we were losing on an hourly basis, here came life in all its glory, yelling her tale to the whole world. *I WILL SURVIVE!*

Just then a doctor arrived. "Can I help?"

I handed him the sweet little girl who had just made her arrival into the world, and I stayed with the mom. I ensured that the placenta had been delivered intact; I massaged her belly to make sure that the uterus was clamping down. As I sat down beside her, I looked at her and we connected at the most intimate level with the shared knowledge of what it meant to be a mom. We smiled, and although we did not speak the same language, the universal language of love was shared between us.

After we both had a chance to catch our breath, the new crew arrived to take over care of this precious cargo. But then came the reality—here I was in Haiti, with no running water, covered in amniotic fluid. Even with all I'd been through, all I had seen, I wasn't relishing the idea of being covered in that for longer than I actually had to. So I went to our team and confiscated every wipe they had brought with them. I felt I had a higher calling to use the wipes than they did, and they agreed. I peeled off my scrubs, washed down with 100 baby wipes, and put my "spare" scrubs on, ready to get a few hours of sleep before our next shift arrived.

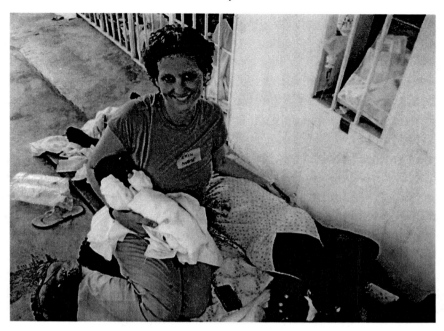

Life had entered the world, and I felt as small as a flea, humbled to be a part of this amazing miracle in the middle of earthquake-torn Haiti. It felt surreal. God had met me and brought me through it. In that moment God was present—in the midst of death, in the midst of chaos, in the midst of destruction—here was life! We had never been abandoned. We were met in our deepest fear and anxiety. He gave me what I needed: the compassion, the strength, the intuition, and the knowledge to make sure mama and baby were fine. I was just a pinky in His great big hand, and He had met me where I was!

"For behold, when the sound of your greeting came to my ears, the baby in my womb leaped for joy." – Luke 1:44

A week later I was still in Haiti, still in the hospital, still running sixteen-hour night shifts. I stepped up as the charge nurse, coordinating patients coming in, staffing, starting IVs, triaging patients, handling emergencies, giving an extra hand, and overseeing the nurses on shift.

In the middle of one very long night, we had an emergency that stood out among the many we had while we were there. A man came to us in respiratory distress. His lips were blue, and he was being dragged in by his friend. The doc and I ran to his aid. We laid him down and grabbed the nearest oxygen tank, only to find that it was completely empty. We grabbed the next one and realized that there was no handle to start the flow of oxygen. One thing I've tried to do over the years is to always be prepared. I realize that the Boy Scouts have a monopoly on this, but I must say—you can't talk to a nurse without knowing that they are prepared for almost any circumstance. I rummaged through my fanny pack and whipped out my Leatherman. Popping open the wrench tool, I opened the oxygen tank.

We put a non-rebreather oxygen mask on this blue-lipped man, and then he completely stopped breathing. The doc and I looked at each other, our eyes wide. I grabbed the nearest ambu-bag and started manually pumping oxygen into this man's lungs. We had no ventilator and very little access to emergency medication, and we knew that we were not going to be able to keep this man alive.

The doc asked if I was okay to continue, and I nodded. He found a local Haitian man and asked if he knew of any other medical facilities that were close by that we could possibly go to. He told him of a U.S. military MASH unit that was on the other side of town—perhaps they could help. So with the help of a few other people around us, we lifted the man into the back of a station wagon and took off.

At 2 a.m., there were no lights on the street. Port-au-Prince was still trying to get back on the grid after the earthquake. People were sleeping on the streets, afraid to go back into their houses for fear that they would collapse on them. There was rubble on the streets and dead bodies that had not made it to the mass gravesite. We sped down the dark roads as fast as we dared, avoiding both living and dead bodies as we raced to the military hospital we hoped was open for business. We prayed as I continued bagging the unresponsive patient.

We pulled up to the massive tent that was the MASH hospital, and our doc went in to talk to the people there while I continued to keep the man alive. Gratefully, the MASH unit was able to take our patient.

They did not have a ventilator either, but they had more staff and fewer patients, so they took our patient and did the best that they could for him.

After another ten days helping out at the hospital, I returned to my normal life in Honduras and left Haiti behind. My life had been changed, there was no denying that. You can't go through experiences like that and not be changed. It is then that you see not only the worst in people, but also the best. When the starving person gives the last food they have to someone else. When the family whose tiny tent is bursting at the seams takes in one more person. When people from all over the world band together to try and make a difference. I pray that God was able to use my hands to lessen the pain of someone who was grieving, to show love to someone who had lost all hope, to bring new life into the world.

"The Spirit of God has made me, and the breath of the Almighty gives me life." – Job 33:4

Chapter 29

Beauty and Trash

"The grass withers, the flower fades, but the word of our God will stand forever." – Isaiah 40:8

In 2012, we finally were able to construct a permanent clinic in the little village of Armenia Bonito. Immediately prior to opening its doors, I interviewed and hired a local Christian Honduran physician. Up until then, I had spent most of my medical time in Honduras running mobile clinics—packing up all my medication, supplies, tables, etc. into the back of my little red truck and hosting clinics in the dump community, at a squatter village beside the river, in a barely functioning kindergarten classroom, under trees, and under tents.

With the opening of the permanent clinic, we didn't want to abandon all the patients we had made over the years in our various mobile clinic locations around town. So, we decided to have the permanent clinic open Tuesday through Friday and maintain a rotating mobile clinic to continue serving our other patients on Mondays. This would also allow us to offer extended and specialty services to our remote sites when we had visiting medical brigades from the States.

During one of these brigades, one of the nurses asked me if I had become blinded to the beauty in Honduras. I looked around me and told her, "Not a chance!" I couldn't possibly grow accustomed to the beauty that surrounded me every day on my drive out to my clinic and the view from my little office.

My clinic in Honduras is called the El Arbol de la Vida—the Tree of Life:

¹Then he showed me a river of the water of life, clear as crystal, coming from the throne of God and of the Lamb, ²in the middle of its street. On either side of the river was the tree of life, bearing twelve kinds of fruit, yielding its fruit every month; and the leaves of the tree were for the healing of the nations. ³There will no longer be any curse; and the throne of God and of the Lamb will be in it, and His bond-servants will serve Him; ⁴they will see His face, and His name will be on their foreheads. ⁵And there will no longer be any night; and they will not have need of the light of a lamp nor the light of the sun, because the Lord God will illumine them; and they will reign forever and ever. – Revelation 22:1-5

I asked the visiting nurse what had prompted her question. She asked me about the beauty first, but she wanted to follow up with a question about the trash. Trash. The collection and disposal of trash in a city can tell you a lot about the state of that city and country. Honduras is overwhelmed with its trash. In Honduras, it is culturally acceptable to throw trash out of windows of the bus and to dump it in collection piles around town where it will never be disposed of. There are areas of the city that are fairly clean, where workers pick up litter. However, there are just as many, if not more, areas where trash has collected and sat for who knows how long.

I come from a country of cleanliness and recycling. In the community outside of Sacramento where we had a home, I was fined by the Home Owners Association because I hadn't brought my trash can inside quickly enough after the trash truck had come collecting. Our grass in the front yard couldn't be taller than one inch, and you were not allowed to paint the outside of your house without approval. Some people may find this type of living confining, but it appealed to my sense of organization and orderliness. I loved the neighborhood we lived in. My view was not polluted with the ugly presence of trash, and I could breathe deeply without encountering the foul stench of rotting trash.

So, the nurse asked me, if you aren't blinded to the beauty, what about the trash? We were sitting outside of one of the mobile clinic locations that we came to all the time, and I looked at her in confusion. "What trash?" I asked.

Her eyes got wide, and she turned her head less than 45 degrees to look at the abandoned building right across the road from where we had set up clinic. "THAT trash," she said. And

it was like my vision went from fuzzy to clear in a second as soon as she pointed it out. *Wow!* That was all I could think. I hadn't even noticed the trash. And we had been coming to this location for months.

And then she asked me about the military and the police. "Oh, those I see because I get stopped all the time." The military with their rifles and machine guns, and the police with riot gear and black masks for the narco cops. But they weren't shocking to me. They were a part of daily life there. But it is shocking when you come from a country where the police and military are working hard and doing their job, but are typically only seen if a need arises.

When we pulled into the community that day, there had been a riot outside on the street, and the police were in full force. The visiting team couldn't stop talking about it—it was the topic of every conversation for quite some time. I had forgotten about it the second we drove past it.

So, that got me thinking. Why had I become blind to the trash and police/ military presence, but not lost the ability to see the beauty in the world. Honestly, I think it came down to priorities and a small sense of self-preservation. Beauty makes me happy—it reminds me of the presence of God and of His creation. It is uplifting. It is humbling. It is the sense of positiveness in all things, even in the darkness of living in the most murderous country in the world. It's Hope. That's why I still see the beauty and not the trash. God brings Hope through His son. And that's what I want to portray to those I serve. The Hope in Him that is beauty.

Even with the constant police and military presence, there were more than 300 murders a year in our own little city of La Ceiba. Living in the most murderous country in the world, we heard about it every day. Once sin entered the world, the first murder occurred. Man is sin. Only in the Hope that is Jesus Christ can humanity come out from under the darkness it is in. So, I choose to see the beauty in the world, to focus on that, while not losing sight of sin. But my priority is the light in the world, not the darkness.

So I think I'm okay with being blind to the trash. I choose not to be a contributor to the casual act of throwing trash out the window. I believe we are to be good stewards of the world and to do our share to keep it clean. But I don't want to become immersed in a world of trash. I don't want to look outside my window and only see debris. I want to see the beauty. I want to see the beauty in people that surround me every day. The beauty of the filthy child with a snotty nose that comes to my clinic and runs up to me to get a hug. But there is one thing I never want to become blind to—the poverty, the starvation, the hunger, the illness, the death that also surround me every day. The day I become blind to it is the day I leave the mission field.

"Finally, brothers and sisters, whatever is true, whatever is noble, whatever is right, whatever is pure, whatever is lovely, whatever is admirable—if anything is excellent or praiseworthy—think about such things." – Philippians 4:8

Chapter 30

Bichos

"Now I rejoice in my sufferings for your sake, and in my flesh I am filling up what is lacking in Christ's afflictions for the sake of his body, that is, the church," – Colossians 1:24

Worms, intestinal parasites, bichos. They became an integral part of my daily life in Honduras. Children wandered around without shoes—some because they didn't want to wear them and some because they couldn't afford them. Flip flops or sandals were the shoe of choice in the hot country of Honduras. However, they really didn't offer much in the way of protection from harm or from the contraction of diseases.

In the villages we worked in there were few homes that had running water. Houses had latrines, or outhouses, outside. Some only offered a hole in the floor, some offered a toilet bowl with no seat, and most were barely enclosed enough to provide any semblance of privacy. Because the latrines only rested over rock-lined holes in the ground, sewage leaked into the surrounding ground and into the water table. Needless to say, the water in most villages was not potable. The La Ceiba health department did an annual assessment of the water in and around the city and found only one community that had potable water from its faucets. The reason that location had potable water was because its water source was set up by a private company.

Communities were taught how to keep their water sources chlorinated and were even provided with chlorine tablets to put in their water storage tanks. However, as the water was carried through the decades-old PVC pipes that brought it into the city, it was contaminated by sewage seepage from the latrines. So water could be potable at the storage tank up on the mountain, but by the time it reached individual households there was nothing potable about it.

The end result was that everyone had worms. The children coughed them up, they pooped them out, and they were severely malnourished because of the parasite load their guts were carrying. They were anemic and underweight.

Eradication of parasitic worms was one of the very first things I wanted to accomplish upon my arrival to the community. Maybe that was just a pipe dream, but I was determined that every single child and adult would get a deworming pill once every six months as recommended by the World Health Organization.

In addition to the deworming pill, I gave out vitamins as I was able to. Every child five and under received a month supply of vitamins. Initially we held vitamin drives at churches back in the States. We asked churches to have their members purchase and bring in tons and tons of adult and children's vitamins. But I just couldn't keep up. Visiting teams would bring them down or we would pay an exorbitant amount to have them shipped down, but I would still run out. That is, until I contacted Vitamin Angels and applied for a grant for children's and prenatal vitamins. And my grant was accepted! We still paid for the shipment, but all of my prenatal and children's vitamins were taken care of. I was ecstatic!

Just handing out vitamins and deworming pills wasn't enough for me, however. Part of my love, my personal mandate, and my moral obligation was health education. While going through nursing school, I began to get a feel for where my passions were leading me. Maternal and child health was the highest on my personal list. Lowest on my list was psychiatric nursing and public health. Those two groups take a very special kind of nurse, and I just didn't think I had it in me. I went through my public health rotation dreading each clinic day. It was a huge burden to me. In my mind, there was ZERO chance I was ever going to be a public health nurse.

Yet here I am now, with more than ten years on the mission field, and what am I? I am a public health nurse. I educate and serve the population at large. I have become what I said I would never be. I create non-reading health education sheets. I give lectures, visit homes, even put on clinics dedicated specifically to vitamin and parasite medication distribution. And to take it a step further, I am finishing up my Masters Degree in Public Health, Population Medicine through Loma Linda University. When I step back and look at where I am and what I've become, trust me, the irony is NOT lost on me.

I would like to think that improvements were made in those villages through my efforts. When I brought a Honduran physician onto the team, I instilled in him the importance of parasite medication. With every visiting medical brigade, I made sure that parasite medication was a standard order. My desire was to see children thrive, to go to bed without the horrible stomach pains of parasitic infestation or severe diarrhea. I hoped to see children's immune systems rebound and anemia subside. Once again, I tried to make a difference, one child at a time.

"Behold, I will bring to it health and healing, and I will heal them and reveal to them abundance of prosperity and security." – Jeremiah 33:6

Chapter 31

Emergency

"The Spirit of God has made me, and the breath of the Almighty gives me life." – Job 33:4

One of our mobile clinics was located in a riverside community that consisted mainly of squatters. I don't mean this in a derogatory sense; it just describes the transient living of the people in this community. The government does not legally recognize this community because it's next to the river and is often flooded during extremely heavy storms. The government does not want people living there because lives are lost each time a huge storm comes through. However, that does not stop the squatters.

The houses are mostly wooden shacks, stick huts with dirt floors and only the electricity they can slave off of from the neighboring community. They have no access to water other than the river, and I would say that less than half of the houses have any type of latrine.

There are about 1,000 people who live here, with many coming and going. The ones going are hopefully going to a more permanent living situation; the ones coming are people who have been pushed out of homes, women leaving hostile environments, and others who have no family members to care for them. It was to this community we came once a month.

I was working with two of my nonmedical teammates. They were helping organize the people waiting—getting intake information and general vital signs, and chatting with people while they waited. As you might imagine, a clinic in this type of setting sees many different types of people. Young and old, pregnant, new babies. Chronic conditions and acute ones—you name it, we see it. Most people know that I may have emergency equipment, but it's only what I can carry in a box, and my resources are limited to say the least. If you have an emergency, it's off to the public hospital you go.

One particular day tested me both physically and emotionally. A family from a neighboring community heard about our free medical clinic and came with their eleven-year-old daughter Wendy, who had a history of asthma. She was doing poorly the day before, but this day she was much worse. She presented to the clinic in obvious respiratory distress. Although it wasn't her turn, I took one look at her and bypassed our normal check-in procedure and put her in front of me for a full assessment.

Her lungs sounded terrible, barely passing air, and a quick check of her oxygen levels showed she was in distress. Her respiratory rate was anywhere from 40-60 breaths per minute, and her heart rate was elevated to over 150 beats per minute. I gave her an inhaler, had her use it, gave her some steroids, and put her on a nebulizer treatment immediately. I frantically looked around for her mom and told her we needed to get her to a hospital immediately! This was NOT the place for this.

I had worked in a pediatric hospital for twelve years, and I had seen my fair share of children in respiratory distress. I was present when an eight-year-old boy was admitted to the Pediatric ICU where he died from an asthma attack. To say that I was worried about Wendy is an understatement. Scared is a much more accurate assessment. My heart was pounding, and my eyes were as big as my patient's. But there I was in this village, with no means of transportation. I was waiting for the mother, who had gone home to get her husband.

I sat with Wendy while she received her breathing treatment. I talked to her calmly, asking her to breathe with me to try and slow her breathing rate, and just talked of simple things to keep her mind elsewhere. Her eyes were as big as saucers as her lungs frantically tried to exchange what little air they could. Slowly but surely, over the next twenty minutes or so (and three breathing treatments later), her little body slowly started to respond. She was breathing less often, her heart rate was slower, her other muscles were relaxing, and her eyes were almost back to normal. I breathed a sigh of relief. I continued to work with her and had my teammate come help me do some chest percussion to help clear her lungs.

By that time her mother had returned. I explained to her that things were much better. But I gave her a stern lesson on never letting her daughter be without an inhaler (she had run out of medication). I gave her an inhaler and told her to return often to make sure she was never without one. Ten minutes later, with continuing monitoring, Wendy was laughing and even coloring some coloring pages I had given her. She had turned the corner.

I sat down, and my hands started shaking. The emergency was over, the adrenaline that had kept me going was running its course. Once again I had found myself on my own to keep this girl medically stable. It was a little overwhelming. I felt tears in the corners of my eyes. I was drained. Living there, I bore the burden of knowing the desperation that these sweet people lived on a day-to-day basis. I shuddered to think what might have happened to that sweet little girl if I had not been there that day. But God knew. He gave me what I needed, and He gave little Wendy what she needed. I let her go with the promise she would return in two weeks when I would be there to follow up with her.

"We must approach God 'in full assurance of faith,' that is, resting fully on the sufficiency of Christ's sacrifice for our sins, not on our good deeds, to gain us access into God's presence."
John MacArthur, The Pillars of Christian Character: The Basic Essentials of a Living Faith (Wheaton, IL: Crossway Books, 1998), 165.

Chapter 32

Roadside Consult

"I was naked and you clothed me, I was sick and you visited me, I was in prison and you came to me." – Matthew 25:36

The police and military presence are just part of the norm when living in Honduras. It gets to the point that you barely process they are there. Private businesses have armed guards that protect their property and belongings, if the owner can afford it, and every bank has at least two shotgun-toting armed guards.

Stolen cars, gun running, drug selling and murder are also a part of everyday living in Honduras. Because of that, there are police checkpoints all throughout the city of La Ceiba. With only one street to get into the city and one street to get out of the city, it's fairly easy for the police to set up these checkpoints, and there really is no way to avoid them. They sit at the bridge of each border river and randomly select cars to pull over. There is no need for a warrant: if they want to search your car, they can. Our car has heavily tinted windows, which make it almost impossible to see inside of the car. We don't want to be targets, so we do as much as possible to blend in with everyone else. It's tough to do when you are a 6'1" tall white woman with tattoos, but we try. I guess the nice thing in all this is that we pretty much don't fit any profile of the above-mentioned criminals. So we roll our windows down when are approaching a police checkpoint, they take one look at us and send us on our way.

As I was on my way back from a mobile clinic one day, I approached one of the normal checkpoints. I dutifully rolled my window down, stuck my arm out the window so they could see I was a woman and white, and was prepared to continue on my way when one of the police officers saw me and pulled me over. My luck had run out. We had encountered a few police officers that were looking for more than our driver's license, but for the most part, the officers really wanted to make a safer city.

The officer that pulled me over had seen that I was wearing scrubs. When he pulled me over, he glanced in the back of my pickup that was full of plastic boxes filled with medical supplies. I was confused and was waiting for the typical questions, "Where are you coming from? Where are you headed? Can I see your registration?" But instead he said to me, "Do you have any medicine for a cough and a cold? And my wife has a cold too. Can you help us out?"

So, what's a girl to do when the police ask? I hopped out of my car, rummaged through my boxes, and pulled out what he needed. I then asked him how many children he had at home, and pulled out enough vitamins to help every child in his home. All in a day's work!

Another roadside consult…another day…

Multiple times a year we brought in medical brigades and took them to the many communities we were working in. On one particular day, I was in the truck with Dr. Greg. Dr. Greg came down to Honduras twice a year since the first year we arrived in Honduras. He is a genius, has developed new medical equipment, has made improvements on existing medical equipment, has run departments, and yet is one of the humblest men I know. He brought a portable ultrasound with him when he came, and he brought his experience, knowledge, expertise and love with him. He found cancer, twins, problematic pregnancies, and was there when we had emergencies. His wife was an incredible supporter of our ministry as well. She always ensured that medications were packed, supplies were received for the trip, and always made sure that all of the missionaries had gifts and fun tastes from home. I often wondered what would happen on each of his trips, because each time something unusual happened. But I would never have expected what happened that day.

There we were, in a caravan of trucks with the whole team, making our way to our first clinic location. My truck had Dr. Greg, my husband, and a few other team members in it. One of the long roads we were traveling down was always very busy with cars, trucks, motorcycles, bicycles and pedestrians. On this particular day we saw a motorcycle making its way down the street. For whatever reason, the motorcyclist swerved, hit some gravel, and went flying off his motorcycle, smacking his head on the curb. This happened directly in front of our truck. I was amazed that we didn't hit him.

I grabbed the box of medical supplies labeled "wound care," and Dr. Greg and I jumped out of the truck. We each put on a pair of gloves and started to assess the man right there on the side of the road. I talked to him in Spanish and was able to ensure that he was (mostly) neurologically intact. He had plenty of road rash from sliding and bouncing along the gravel and road, but amazingly was mostly okay. If he had not been wearing his helmet, the story would have ended very differently.

With shaking hands, he called his wife to tell her what happened. He sat there with a dazed look on his face, but was oddly calm as he knew we were there to help him. We cleaned all of his road rash areas and the gash in his arm, and Dr. Greg gave him a good overall physical. We prayed for this man and expressed how much we cared for him. We put together a little care package of additional bandages, cleaning supplies and plenty of Tylenol as we knew his pain would be coming.

I often wonder what God is going to put in front of my path each day, but I didn't realize that day would be a literal "I am putting one of my children in front of you today, and want you to care for him" kind of moment.

Chapter 33

A Toad on my Shoe

"Then Noah built an altar to the Lord and took some of every clean animal and some of every clean bird and offered burnt offerings on the altar." – Genesis 8:20

I am one of those people who has a heart for all things living. If there is a spider in my house, I carefully collect it and help it find its way outside where it can do more good. I like animals. I like insects. I am a catch-and-release kind of girl. Get the picture? My earliest memory is from preschool. I found a baby bird that had fallen from its nest, and I took it to the teachers because I knew it must be saved!

I once rescued a mouse from a sticky trap at the prison I worked in. It was a big prison, and old, so mice were a common occurrence. But if you are going to kill a mouse, kill a mouse. To capture it on a sticky trap and let it suffer just gets me at my core. So, I spent an HOUR unsticking the mouse from the trap and letting it go in the field across from us. Of course, my husband was gracious enough to tell me that he was sure that an owl had had it for dinner that night.

I spent nine years in the military, and one day on my way to formation a bird hit my car. I got out of my car, took my uniform top off, collected the bird, and took it to a wildlife rescue center. Yeah, I was late to formation—try explaining THAT one to your 1st Sergeant.

Well, I have a heart for ALMOST all things living. Honduras is a rain forest country. I know I've said that before, but it is worth repeating. Because along with the jungle, and the rain, there are going to be critters. And some critters—I'm just going to say it—don't belong in my house. I don't know how they get in. I just don't get it.

One morning as I was making my way downstairs my eyes lit on our shoe pile at the foot of the stairs. I was a little bleary-eyed; I'm just not really a morning person. In my sleepy stupor, I could not believe what I saw there. Staring up at me with the most innocent look on its face was a toad. Now I'm not talking a frog; I'm talking a TOAD! This ginormous monstrosity of a thing was sitting there and staring at me. It even managed to give its equivalent of a middle finger and croaked at me! If I can to guess, I would say that this toad was probably the size of both the palms of my hands put together.

I looked at Mr. Toad and thought all sorts of not-so-nice thoughts. But then my mind settled on the most pressing matter—how in the WORLD had this giant-sized toad made its way into my house? And what other kind of creature could make its way through the same huge entryway! I felt like I must have had a neon sign above the entrance that this monstrosity entered, and I was totally convinced that an anaconda was then going to make its way in and eat this toad while I stood there looking at it.

Once my bleary eyes had focused and my mind had wrapped itself around this unfortunate incident, I thought about what to do next. There was no chance this toad was staying in my house, and I wasn't about to pick him up with my bare hands. You see, these kind of toads give off a milky substance that is poisonous. That is their one defense mechanism that prevents other creatures from eating them. I went into the kitchen, grabbed a garbage bag, scooped up Mr. Toad and took him outside to the empty field right next to us. Yeah, even though I was not fond of Mr. Toad, I know how many other critters he eats and takes care of, so he deserved to live out his life taking care of business—just not in MY house.

Another day…another critter…

My husband was gone for the evening, and my daughter was spending the weekend at her friend's house, so I had the house to myself. During this quiet, peaceful night, my world was about to change.

When we lived in Honduras, we had two very sweet 100-pound Rottweilers. They were quite the hunters. Most of the time our house was rat- and mouse-free because they caught them. They were wicked fast, and actually hunted together as a pair. One flushed out the prey, and the fast one caught it. It was quite amazing to watch. But even they didn't want anything to do with what I found that night.

I was sitting on the couch, watching TV, when I got the feeling that something was watching me. The hair on the back of my neck rose, the feeling so strong that even my steady nerves were tested. So I slowly scanned the room, searching out the thing that was looking at me, and there it sat in all its eight-legged hairiness. Not a tarantula, but one of the biggest spiders I had ever seen. This thing could have featured in a late-night horror flick. I jumped off of the couch, and suddenly ALL the hairs on my arms and neck—heck, I think even my eyebrows—were standing on edge. It was just disgusting! There was ZERO chance I was going to be able to sleep that night, much less stay in my house if I knew that that thing was still around.

The first thing I did was to grab my camera to document it in all its disgustingness. I knew no one would believe how awful that thing was unless I showed them proof. It would be like that fish story that everyone likes to tell: "No, really, I caught a TEN FOOT Salmon!"

So how was I going to get rid of this monstrosity? It had the nerve to be sitting nonchalantly on the door frame of my front door. So opening the front door was out. Taking a deep breath, I came up with a plan. Our house was a little oddly constructed. Right next to our front door there was a set of double doors as well. I'm not sure what brought about that strange configuration, but it was going to provide me with just the critter eviction I needed.

So as not to scare the giant (although I'm positive this was not one of those "he's really more scared than I am" moments, because he could clearly eat me in one bite), I gently tiptoed to the broom that was propped against the wall. Then I ever-so-smoothly eased over to the double doors to open them when the most horrible thing happened—it jumped! I'm not talking like a run or a little movement; it seriously jumped about ten feet and ran under the couch I had previously been sitting on.

In that moment, it was almost like I was watching a movie of myself. I was laughing and freaking out, in 100% determined amazon-woman mode. There was no way this thing was going to get away from me and stay in my house. I was a mad woman—I grabbed the couch and literally flung it to the side. Out ran the spider—to the other couch. So I sprinted to that couch and flung it aside, and out it ran again. Then it stopped and looked at me with all 100 of its eyes. With the whole jumping episode fresh in my mind, it was clear to me what could possibly happen. It was a fight or flight moment—not for the spider, for me! But as so often happens, the fighter in me came out. So with my broom lowered to the floor and the set of double doors behind the enemy, I made like a hockey player getting ready to make the winning shot. I hit for the win.

Out if flew—straight through the strategically-placed double doors—and skittered off into the night. My heart was pumping, my breathing was labored, but I had survived. I had been triumphant!

Chapter 34

Intruder

The thief comes only to steal and kill and destroy. I came that they may have life and have it abundantly." – John 10:10

It's days like this that just make you grumpy.

A normal day, a normal routine. We had a twenty-person team visiting and working with us. I was down at the clinic with some members of the team when Mike called me from home. Our house had been completely ransacked. We had been robbed.

There are a lot of reactions that can come after an announcement like that. Anger, sadness, frustration, loss. I felt all of those, pretty much all at the same time. I had a lot of questions for Mike. *Where was the dog? Is he okay? Are you okay?*

To get into our house took a whole lot of effort. First of all, there was the dog. At this point in time we only had one, but he was 100-pounds worth of Rottweiler. To know him was to love him, but to an average Honduran, he looked like a vicious guard dog. In Honduras, only one type of person owns a dog like ours, and that's the local drug lords who want to guard their property. So, most Hondurans are terrified of coming to our gate once they see what is on the other side. The second thing you have to get through is our ten-foot-high gate with razor wire across the top. Then there was the solid wood door at the front of the house with three sets of locks.

It was an "inside job"—there was no other explanation. Someone knew we weren't going to be there. They knew our dog, and the dog knew them. No Honduran would dare to hop our fence if he didn't know our dog.

They were looking for items of value. So our DVD player was gone, along with Mike's computer, and any other electronic device they could carry off. We didn't have our permanent medical clinic yet, so all of my medications and supplies were stored at our house. Obviously, the robber had no idea what to do with all of it, but decided they wanted to be sure we weren't hiding anything, so they dumped the entire closet full of medication and supplies onto the floor. Our house was a MESS! Nothing was left untouched.

Thankfully we are good at hiding things. So, our guns, our passports, and our cash hadn't been touched. And the rest—well, the rest was "just" electronics, and a complete mess that had to be cleaned up.

As Mike was giving me the update, I must have gone through the stages of grief in about five minutes. Once I took in all that Mike had told me, I started crying as I imagined what a mess my house was in. Then I got mad. Really mad. Like seeing red kind of mad. Then I got to acceptance, because what can you do? I lived in the murder capital of the world, in the second poorest country in the western hemisphere. People are desperate. So, that's where I sat, balanced between anger and acceptance.

We got a new front door and an additional security door in front of that. We put additional razor wire across the top of the fence and hoped for the best. We had been invaded, but our family was safe. The things that mattered were still intact—our dog was alive and healthy, and our family was none the worse for wear.

I realize the enemy doesn't like where we are; he doesn't like that we are working for the right team. He will find ways to try and get underneath us and rattle our foundation. But when we live on a solid foundation, no storm that comes can rock our boat. Our first pastor told us (and I paraphrase): How sad are the lives of people who never have adversity—that Satan cares so little for what they are doing that he doesn't bother them. So rejoice when adversity comes, because we hold onto Him who is able to do all things, and we fight on!

Chapter 35

I am not responsible FOR you, I am responsible TO you

"Trust in the Lord with all your heart, and do not lean on your own understanding." – Proverbs 3:5

These words I have taken to heart.

The first day Mike and I set foot in the small 3,000 person community of Armenia Bonito in the jungles of Honduras, we were overwhelmed with what we encountered there—the despair, poverty, substandard living situations, and health conditions. And it was easy to succumb to the immensity of it. But the words in Proverbs hounded me.

There are more than 2,000 references in the Bible related to children and poverty.

"Defend the cause of the weak and fatherless; maintain the rights of the poor and oppressed. Rescue the weak and needy; deliver them from the hand of the wicked." – Psalm 82:3-4

"If anyone has material possessions and sees his brother in need but has no pity on him, how can the love of God be in him? Dear children, let us not love with words or tongue but with actions and in truth." – 1 John 3:17-18

Interestingly, when I returned to work on the pediatric oncology floor of the hospital while on furlough, I found that these words spoke to me just as deeply. In every room I entered was a child afflicted with cells that were growing out of control, taking over their little bodies. I was either desperately trying to save them from a severe infection by giving them lifesaving antibiotics or pumping poison into their veins with chemotherapy to try and stop the spread of those out-of-control cells. I walked into the rooms of children who had no hair on their heads, who were throwing up into buckets while their parents sat helplessly holding their frail little bodies as they groaned in agony.

I rallied myself at each and every room to put on the face I needed to: the one of compassion, yet the one of efficiency; the face of kindness, yet the mindset of getting my job done. I had to continue in my endeavor to care for those little ones who had been entrusted to me, and yet not lose it when the little five-year-old girl with just a wisp of hair looked at me with her big eyes and asked if she was going to be okay. Because the truth was, I just didn't know.

To find that very narrow road and walk it with integrity, mercy, and efficiency was a difficult task indeed. Having enough compassion to not be frustrated when you have given all the medications you can possibly give and yet still see a sweet child suffering. To somehow be okay, knowing that you have done the best that you could do.

Because to go down the wide road, to take on all the burdens that have been laid before you, means you will not be able to walk down that road again and again, day after day after day.

Working on an oncology floor and working on the mission field present so many similarities. I never made the connection before I went to Honduras, but the despair, loneliness, hopelessness can seem much the same.

To give a sliver of hope—a light in the darkness, a compassionate smile and a hug to those who are suffering—is what gives me the ability to go on from day to day. I never realized before how much the job of a hospital nurse and the role of a missionary nurse in a third world country overlap.

But to maintain my strength to go on from day to day, I can't take that last step into the depth of despair with that child, with that family, with that diagnosis or station in life because I wouldn't be able to climb back out to be able to look after the next family, the next child, the next situation. After all, I am not responsible FOR that person, I am only responsible TO that person.

As I looked back over my work at the hospital and at the overwhelming poverty and despair of Honduras, I wrote out these words to rally my heart and to remind myself. My job is this...

To be obedient to God:

Therefore go and make disciples of all nations, baptizing them in the name of the Father and of the Son and of the Holy Spirit Matthew 28:19.

He has led me here:

Then I heard the voice of the Lord saying, "Whom shall I send? And who will go for us?" And I said, "Here am I. Send me!" - Isaiah 6:8

He will not fail me:

The LORD himself goes before you and will be with you; he will never leave you nor forsake you. Do not be afraid; do not be discouraged - Deuteronomy 31:8

He will equip me:

[20]Now the God of peace, who brought up from the dead the great Shepherd of the sheep through the blood of the eternal covenant, [21]even Jesus our Lord, equip you in every good thing to do His will, working in us that which is pleasing in His sight, through Jesus Christ, to whom be the glory forever and ever. Amen. Hebrews 13:20-21

Chapter 36

So What DOES $25 Buy?

"For I was hungry and you gave me food, I was thirsty and you gave me drink, I was a stranger and you welcomed me,"
– Matthew 25:35

My dad came to Honduras not long after my mother passed away. He had always wanted to come and was trying to figure out how to get my mother, who was very disabled, to come down as well. In the end, she was never able to come, but after she passed, my dad came down – three times!

On the first of these trips, I needed to go to the grocery store to buy some things for the house, and my dad came along. We went to a local store, and I picked up two grocery carts. I started filling both carts, and my dad finally stopped me and asked what I was doing. I explained to him that one of my outreach ministries was to provide food baskets for the very poor. Unfortunately, that description fits most of the community in the village we work in. However, there was a certain criteria that those families had to meet in order to be eligible to receive a food basket. Typically, we would receive information from one of the local churches that there was a family in distress. We met with them, assessed their situation, and then provided the basket of food for them. It was truly the basics with no frills. But it was enough to sustain a small family for about a month.

My dad then asked me how much money I spent on each food basket. I told him that I limited it to $25, but that amount of money would give the family the basics of what they needed.

He was shocked. He looked at me and asked me again, "Twenty-five dollars will feed a family for a month?"

"Yes," I told him, with no extras and no frills.

He responded, "I'm all in!"

I looked at him in confusion.

He said, "I know I'm supporting you guys financially every month, but I want to send separate money each month for you to buy a food basket for a needy family."

What an awesome gift! So for the next four years he did just that. It was such a small thing, a simple thing, and yet a life-sustaining thing. We gave them out to families that were starving, who had no resources, to widows and orphans. We didn't give to the same family more than once, as we didn't want to form any kind of dependency, but we wanted to help a family when, for them, there was no help to be found.

A typical food basket consisted of corn flour, wheat flour, salt, sugar, pasta, spaghetti sauce, cornflakes, oil, shortening, powdered milk, rice, beans, sugar, chicken bullion, baking soda, chlorine, dish soap, laundry soap, and napkins.

While my dad was there he was able to see his ministry in action. A sweet young woman in the community was a widow and a mom. Her husband had been killed a year earlier by a gang for the $10 he had in his pocket. Needless to say, she was barely been getting by, and was currently without food of any kind in her home. Her name was Elida and she lived with her one-and-a-half-year-old son in a tiny little room. She was very blessed by the basket we were able to provide to her, and we were blessed to be able to give it!

"Happy is the generous man, the one who feeds the poor." –
Proverbs 22:9

Chapter 37

Doctora Teresa

"Heal the sick, cleanse the lepers, raise the dead, cast out devils: freely you have received, freely give." – Matthew 10:8

My first name is Erin, but my mother, in her wisdom, chose Teresa as my middle name. I must say, I was never a fan of my middle name, but let's face it—how many of us actually use our middle names? However, in a Spanish-speaking country, most people had never heard of and had difficulty saying my first name, Erin. My middle name, on the other hand, was very common and easy for them to say, so Teresa it was. I must admit, it really did sound much better with a Spanish accent. As many times as I told the villagers where I worked that I was a nurse, in their eyes it didn't matter. I was "Doctora Teresa."

Nursing is what I have always wanted to do. I want to spend time with people, to listen to their needs and problems, to be a shoulder to cry on. People in Honduras came to me with normal stuff—aches, pains, parasites, wounds that needed cleaning, ear infections, high blood pressure, diabetes. But I also had to stretch myself. I had to become something more than what I was. I wasn't afraid to say, "I don't know," and direct them somewhere else. I also wasn't afraid to tell them like it is. Patient education was not a common thing there. I equated it to the 1950s in the U.S.—you went to the doctor, he told you what pills to take, and you took them. You didn't ask questions, you didn't receive education, you nodded your head, and went on your way. It's what I found in Honduras as well.

One of our workers who did construction at one of our properties had a mild stroke. He went to the doctor and they did not do any immediate care; they gave him ibuprofen and an antibiotic and sent him on his way. When I asked him what the doctor told him to do, he said, "He told me to take these pills."

"Nothing else?" I asked.

"No."

I looked at this sweet man, who was nicknamed "Stomach" (he was HUGE), and knew I needed to step in. I devised a simple change of lifestyle plan for him and his family. He drank anywhere from two to four liters of Coke a day. It was all I ever saw him with, and he ate more tortillas and bagged chips than anyone I had ever seen. I told him I would monitor his blood pressure and blood sugar (both of which were high), and try and get him on a path to wellness. But I also told him if he didn't change his lifestyle, he would die from this.

That was my job. Meeting people at their level. Being the village doctor. Praying with and for them. Educating pregnant young mothers on how to have a healthy pregnancy and a healthy baby. Loving them as a whole.

One week a young woman came to see me. She had a fairly bad urinary tract infection. She had already been to the doctor and had received medication, but she admitted that she stopped taking it because it made her feel weak. After almost thirty minutes of conversation, some loving, and then some severe lecturing, I told her, "I love this community, I love the people here, and I am grateful that you came by today. But the only way I can help you is if you help yourself. You must care for your body. You must have more than one glass of fluid in a day. You must eat vegetables. And you MUST take your medication."

She looked at me so perplexed. I don't think anyone had ever told her that she had the ability to take control of her life and to be proactive in her own health. I don't think anyone had ever taken the time just to listen to her. Then I prayed with her, I kissed her on the cheek, and gave her some more medication with a promise that she would drink more water and take her meds.

Being "Doctora Teresa" brought with it a huge level of responsibility. I had finally gained trust in the community, and most people would listen to my instructions and advice when I gave it to them. After four years of doing nothing but mobile clinics, we finally had our permanent clinic. We started seeing patients, and our "regulars" were diligently coming every month for blood pressure and blood sugar check-ups and renewal of their medications.

At our one year anniversary of the permanent clinic, I told our Honduran medical staff that I wanted to have a celebration. We would have cake and coffee. We would recognize our "star" patients—those who had continued to come and get their monthly medication. We would give small gifts to our oldest and our youngest patients. You get the picture.

So the day came, the cake was made, and I read my speech. I was choked up. I was amazed at all God had done to make this a reality. I was stunned that God has used me, just a nurse, to open up a medical clinic in the jungles of Honduras. It was humbling. I finished my speech, and one of our "regulars" approached me and asked if she could speak to those who had come. I looked at the more than 100 people who had gathered for this event and swallowed nervously. I won't deny it—I was a little worried. What would she say? I stepped aside, and allowed her to take the stage. I thought perhaps she would talk about the good medical care she received, or the medication that was saving her life (with her high blood pressure and high blood sugar), or about the location or hours of the clinic. I was also afraid that she would talk for an hour—the Latin culture does not highlight time, they highlight community. So speaking for a long time would not be unheard of. But I took a deep breath and waited to hear what she had to say.

She said, "You know why I come to THIS clinic? Because Jesus is here." And she sat down.

That was it. I honestly couldn't have scripted anything better. The tears came to my eyes because she got it! Yes, people come to receive good medical care, good physicians, good medicine, but the bottom line was that I wanted to make sure that people could come and meet Jesus here—that we would be different from other clinics and other facilities.

That we would be shining The Truth and His love in everything that we did, and I guess we did, because "Jesus is here."

"For where two or three are gathered in my name, there am I among them." – Matthew 18:20

Chapter 38

The Consequences of Diabetes

"Dear friend, I pray that you may enjoy good health and that all may go well with you, even as your soul is getting along well" - 3 John 1:2.

I LOVE Honduran food. What's not to like? Tortillas and beans, rice and chicken, and Coke. What is noticeable, though, is the absence of fruits and vegetables. If you go to a "tipico" restaurant and order food, the things that will arrive are beans, plantains, and lots of meat. There won't be a fruit or vegetable in sight. And Coke...oh Coke...Now don't get me wrong, I like a Coke (or in my case, Coke Zero) just like the next person, but here it is a way of life. People don't drink water; their fluid of choice is Coke. Children as young as two years old are introduced to a cup of coffee with two tablespoons of sugar in it and Coke.

Unfortunately, this type of diet leads to obesity and Type II diabetes. If a patient comes to my clinic and is over the age of forty, I automatically test their blood sugar. The surprise comes if it ISN'T elevated. There are some pretty serious complications to living with diabetes as any diabetic will tell you. In a country like Honduras with its severe poverty, un-potable water, and unhealthy diet, it's a recipe for diabetic disaster. In addition, very basic medication is given out at the public hospital, but good (expensive) medications are not given out there. Those the patient has to buy. With the cost of medication anywhere from $50 - $150 a month, that leaves the average Honduran totally unable to afford it. So by the time people make it to my clinic, if they have been diabetic for a while, I have a lot of work to do.

I previously mentioned the lack of health education. General education such as what to eat and what not to eat, a balanced diet, the inclusion of water and elimination of Coke in their lives are some of those things. Increasing exercise, and decreasing packaged food is also part of the education. And thankfully, because of the huge support we receive from physicians in the States, we can provide good medicine, medicine that actually has the potential to control their diabetes.

A sweet forty-two-year-old woman came to my clinic one week. Her primary complaint was about a sore on the bottom of her toe. This was the first time I had seen her, so I needed to get some history. She was diabetic and had been for a number of years. But as she had been a patient of the public hospital, she only had some basic medications, and those only when they were actually available. Often she would go to the hospital for medication and they would be out of it, so she was without. I brought her to my exam room and sat her up on the exam table to take a look at that toe.

The first thing I noticed was that her second toe had already been amputated as a complication of her diabetes. The doctors had recommended amputating her entire foot to stem the problem. She was terrified that at the age of forty-two she was at risk for losing her entire foot. Now, I'm not an expert, but the foot seemed pretty salvageable to me, but I wasn't sure that toe was. Because of the medical advice she had received from the local public hospital she did not want to return there. She told me that she simply wouldn't go back there unless there was absolutely no hope. She told me that she had heard about our clinic from one of her friends, so she came to see if I could help. She said to me, "You are one of the sweetest people I know, and I know that you can save it."

Okay, no pressure there!

The first thing I wanted to do was to give her some patient education. I gave her a food journal, and we talked about diet. She had eaten nothing but tortillas and orange juice for breakfast. We talked about the differences between carbohydrates and proteins, and how they affect the body and her blood sugar levels. She soaked it all in. She had never heard any of the information I was telling her before. I told her that I would help her, but that she needed to come to the clinic daily. That way I could evaluate her blood sugars, clean her wound daily, and monitor her situation. With antibiotics, vitamins, and good blood sugar meds, I was hopeful.

A month into the process, the result was more than I could have hoped for. Her toe had totally healed, her blood sugar was under control, and she had a very good understanding of how she could take control of her disease.

Another diabetic came to my clinic about a month later. This woman lived in Roatan, one of the Honduran Bay Islands in the Caribbean, an hour-and-a-half ferry ride from our city and then another hour-and-a-half to my clinic by bus. She had heard about us from some friends. It was amazing how word had spread!

We talked about her health history and how this wound came to be. She told me that she was a diabetic who had chosen not to take medications for personal reasons. She had been diabetic for six years. With no change in lifestyle and refusing to take any medication, it was inevitable that something bad was going to happen; it was just a matter of time. She had gone to see a physician on the island, and he told her that there was nothing he could do. She needed to go to the mainland and seek help at the public hospital. The public hospital took one look at her and told her she needed to have her foot amputated. She didn't go back. That was when she decided to come see us.

I looked at the wound. I honestly didn't even know where to start. The smell coming from her foot, the oozing of bodily fluids from it, and the multiple holes in it left me a little dumbfounded. I took out my wound care supplies and began the process of cleaning around her foot. I filled a syringe with iodine and started to irrigate the hole in the bottom of her foot. But as I did so, iodine started coming out from two spots between her toes. The wound had tunneled under her skin.

At this point, I sat back in my chair and made a pact with her. First, she must come to the clinic every day so I could assess her blood sugars and re-clean and pack her wound. Second, if at any point things started to look worse, she would have to go back to the public hospital (where they would likely amputate her foot). Third, if she took her meds and came in for daily cleanings, but there was no improvement after a month, then I would no longer see her, and she would have to go back to the public hospital. She took in all I was telling her. She got a little mad, I could tell. But ultimately, she agreed to all conditions. So I started her on multiple antibiotics, vitamins, a cleaning and packing regimen, and a diet change. I gave her a cane to take some of the pressure off of her foot when she walked.

She came diligently, and diligently I washed, cleaned, and packed that wound. But nothing was changing. One day about three weeks into this process, I began irrigating her wound and the iodine came out in an additional location.

"Okay, that's it," I told her, "I'm done. We can't do this any longer. Your foot is not getting better, and now I can say it is getting worse. It continues to tunnel, and now there is a new spot. I have given it my best, but my best is not making a difference."

She was mad. "It hasn't been a month!" she said, "I still have a week!"

But I reminded her we had agreed that if it got worse, then she would have to go to the public hospital. She sat up, anger written across her face. I had failed her.

I conceded to a compromise. "Okay, I tell you what. Next week we have a medical brigade coming, and a lot of physicians are on the team. You come in, speak to them, and see what they tell you. That's all I'll offer, but it is against my conscience to treat you any more," I told her.

"FINE," she said, and off she went.

Monday morning, bright and early on Day One of the medical brigade, there she was. I spoke to one of our docs and asked him if there was any way he could use his ultrasound as a diagnostic tool for this woman. I told him what had transpired, what my attempts had failed to accomplish, and he agreed. He asked me about my course of treatment, and said that everything I had done was what he too would have done. So I brought her in, and he looked at her foot. He took the ultrasound and scanned her entire foot, looking for blood circulation.

"Here is the problem, he said. "There is almost no blood circulation getting to this area of her foot. That is why the antibiotics and treatment are doing absolutely nothing for her. There is no hope."

I looked at her, and we talked about what all of this meant. It meant that I was taking her out of my care, and that I would no longer see her. She absolutely must go to the public hospital and see the doctors there. She looked at me again, so very angry because she knew that it meant her foot would be amputated. She had trusted and relied upon me to fix her, even though I had been up-front with her from the beginning that I might not be able to help her. She still had assumed that it was all going to work out.

She got off the table, grabbed her cane, and walked out. I never saw her again.

"Do not be anxious about anything, but in everything, by prayer and petition, with thanksgiving, present your requests to God. And the peace of God, which transcends all understanding, will guard your hearts and your minds in Christ Jesus" – Philippians 4:6-7

Chapter 39

Going to the Dump

"27Do not withhold good from those to whom it is due, when it is in your power to act. 28Do not say to your neighbor, "Come back tomorrow and I'll give it to you"—when you already have it with you." – Proverbs 3:27-28

At the top of the hill lies the city dump. It is there the trucks go twice a week to dump out all the refuse from the city and outlying villages. The city does not have any type of recycling program, but there are a few entrepreneurial individuals that sort through the trash and pull out the plastic and aluminum and anything else they feel can be resold. Everything else finds its way into the dump. Fertilizer containers with leftover fertilizer, oil containers, batteries—you name it—whatever type of toxic waste you can think of makes its way into the dump as there is nowhere else to put it.

On the hillside of the dump is an entire community. They actually sit on top of the old landfill that was buried over, before the new one was built right above them. So when the torrential rains hit that landfill and the water fills it, it then runs off into the community. When water passes through solids or toxins, and picks up part of that toxin, it's called leachate. That is the water that pours into the community after a rainstorm. In other words, the people in this community are living in a state of toxic waste.

It is in this community that my friend works. After he had been working there for about a year, he asked a favor of me. He asked if I would put on a mobile clinic for the people living there. Without hesitation, I said yes.

My first job was to go and assess the community. I needed to do a community walk. This would allow me to see what living there was like. Did they have latrines, running water, electricity, refrigeration? How did they cook and prepare food? How and where did their babies sleep? Was there a school, any access to shops? Taking all these things into account would give me a good idea of what the potential health needs were going to be.

There really wasn't anything that stood out to me that day. I saw mostly normal kinds of clinic stuff. A twenty-two-year-old mother with six children, ear infections, high blood pressure, wound care, stitches, gastric worm infestations, malnutrition, etc. We saw over sixty patients that day and handed out a whole lot of medication. A typical medical clinic cost about $200; this day was more like $400. But the needs were great, and these folk never had an opportunity to go to doctor's office. Their days were full of collecting water, making food, collecting firewood for their outside campfires, and finding ways to make some meager money in town. Getting medication and being seen by a medical provider were luxuries that most of them didn't have.

This was a great opportunity to work in a new community and meet new people. We prayed with all our patients, played with kids, and our friend was able to make some new contacts. When I finished for the day and was packing up, I took a moment to reflect on life here in the dump. I wondered at the desperation that the majority of these folks lived in. As far as places to live, this was close to the worst of the worst. It seemed like a hopeless kind of life, a desperate kind of life, a life where you waded through toxic runoff every day. I was reminded, for probably the thousandth time, of the life that God had given to me and that I wanted to use every day in the best way I could to care for His people.

"The Lord is a refuge for the oppressed, a stronghold in times of trouble." – Psalm 9:9

Chapter 40

Payment for Services Rendered

"¹²For he will deliver the needy who cry out, the afflicted who have no one to help. ¹³He will take pity on the weak and the needy and save the needy from death. ¹⁴He will rescue them from oppression and violence, for precious is their blood in his sight." – Psalm 72:12-14

There is a debate within the mission community and the Non-Governmental Organization (NGO) groups about giving things away for free. Some people feel that as a missionary, you should not charge for anything. Some of the organizations we work with feel the same way. For many years I held a mobile medical clinic in different communities and didn't charge anything. After a short amount of time a couple of things happened. One, I would arrive for the day to start clinic and over a hundred people would be waiting for me. Two, people did not value the free things I was giving out. So, I began to pray and solicit advice from other missionary physicians and hospitals that had been around for a while. The first thing I noticed was that pretty much everyone charged a fee to be seen. And the second thing was that most were still run by North American doctors and nurses.

One of the biggest things I wanted to do was to work myself out of a job. I wanted a Honduran physician and a Honduran nurse to be running the permanent and mobile clinics. But how could I do this with the way things were currently being run? The Honduran government sets the wage for employees all across the board—from day laborers, to teachers, to doctors, all the way up to senators. So one thing I didn't have any control over was the salary to pay my Honduran doctor and nurse.

The communities we worked in were very poor. If the people had jobs, it was as day laborers, otherwise they got by with selling firewood, washing clothes, or as house help for someone in town. There was no way I could charge my patients what I would need to charge to pay for my staff. My purpose was, after all, to serve the very poor. But I also wanted to give them quality medicine and excellent health care. In addition, I didn't want a North American running the clinic; I wanted this to be their clinic. So where was the balance? How could I make it happen?

I realized that most NGOs in the United States survive from the gracious hearts of other people. They aren't there to make money and are not sustainable without generous donations from supporters. So that's what I would do. I raised support for my doctor's salary.

Once that was done, I still needed to make a decision about what I would do for patients coming to the clinic. I had already seen that people did not place any value on things they got for free. I gave out free reading glasses, only to have the same person come back the next week asking for another pair because they had lost them, or sat on them, or gave them away. I had people coming to the clinic for free Tylenol for the pain that would come "next week," and because they were taking up my time and resources, I didn't end up seeing the person with really high blood pressure.

I checked around the city, the public hospital, and the private doctor's offices to get a range of prices for a consult. The public hospital was about five dollars. A specialist, like a pediatrician, was about twenty-five. And private physicians and clinics would range anywhere from one hundred dollars on up.

The other thing I took into account was the cost of food and resources. When assessing the average Honduran, I noticed a common thread with almost every family. They drank soda—a lot of soda—each family had one to two liters of soda each day. There, I thought, was my price. I would charge what it would cost a family to purchase their daily soda. If they could buy that every day, they certainly could use those funds for something more important like their health. The price was set: $2.50 to be seen. The effects were immediate. Gone were the people who were coming to take advantage of the free stuff, and out came the people who truly needed help.

But what about the person or family who couldn't afford even that? I still wanted people to be responsible for their own health. I wanted them to place value on their time and the time of my staff. So, we would ask for an egg or an avocado. We even asked a gentleman to just go outside of the building and pick up trash. I have never and will never turn a patient away because of their inability to pay. But I do want them to value themselves and value what they are receiving, so payment in tamales or flowers is fine by me. I experienced what it was probably like in the early history of our nation. Physicians receiving payment in apple pies, chickens, and the like. And honestly, I liked that.

⁵Who is like the Lord our God, the One who sits enthroned on high, ⁶who stoops down to look on the heavens and the earth? ⁷He raises the poor from the dust and lifts the needy from the ash heap; ⁸he seats them with princes, with the princes of his people. – Psalm 113:5-8

Chapter 41

Hymns and Highwaymen

"He who dwells in the shelter of the Most High will abide in the shadow of the Almighty. [2]I will say to the Lord, My refuge and my fortress, my God, in whom I trust." – *Psalm 91:1-2*

A couple of ladies from our team and I took five young ladies from the village we were working in out to a concert at one of the local churches. We had done a few things like this, trying to give some of the kids a chance to get away from their little village and do something they wouldn't normally do. We had organized outings for groups of sixty to visit the ocean, go to lunch, and play. We had taken boys to local soccer games and put on soccer tournaments. This was an extra special kind of trip. The church we had been attending was going to put on a big Christian concert. This was a huge event, and we had to buy tickets a week in advance to even get in. It was unusual for the girls to get to be out at night. Almost no one in the village had a car, and as taxis won't go into this community after dark and the busses stop running at dusk, there really was no opportunity or way to be out of the village after dark.

We picked the girls up in the village and took them out to dinner. Eating out at a restaurant was an experience that most of them had not had. After dinner, it was off to the church for the concert. The girls had a great time—singing out loud, being silly, just being kids! The concert was two hours long, so it was pretty dark by the time we left. The other members of my team were in one car, and I had the girls from the village in the other. So the other car headed back into town, and I took the girls back to the village.

On my way out to the village, I tried to call Mike and let him know that we were done at the concert and I was taking the girls back home. But the cell phone service wasn't working. This wasn't all that unusual. There were no emergency crews to fix the towers; you typically had to wait until the following day for things to work again. Once in a while you could get a text through if your call wouldn't go through, so I tried texting him multiple times. One of the girls in the car had a phone, so I asked if I could use her phone, but to no avail. There was nothing to do but to just keep going.

pulled off the main road and headed toward the inner part of the village. There were no street lights, and the houses that had electricity were few and far between. The village was about two-and-a-half miles off of the main road, up in the rain forest. There was only one road into the town and only one road out.

I was more than a mile down this unpaved, unlit, jungle road when I noticed it. I was being followed. Two motorcycles. They were keeping their distance, but they were keeping pace with me. Fresh in my mind was a recent incident that had happened to some of our team members. They had been on their way out to the village on this same road when they were followed by two motorcycles and held up at gun point—and that had been in the middle of the day. I knew I was in trouble. All the girls in the car were silent; they knew we were in trouble as well. There was one portion of the road where there was a split: you could go either way to get to the village, it was basically just a big circle. It wouldn't give me a chance to escape, but it gave them a chance—they split up. One went right, and the other stayed behind me. They were going to try to trap me. I knew this in an instant, so I gunned it. I needed to get ahead of the motorcycle that had split off. If they trapped me, I had no idea what they would do to us.

One thing I've always been meticulous about is prevention. I always get our family in for our biannual dentist appointments, annual physicals, and flu shots. I was no different with our car. I had the oil changed every 5,000 miles, got an annual tune-up, replaced the shocks, etc., so I knew my little car could do it. It was only a two-wheel drive, four cylinder, but she was healthy and I knew her well. So I floored it.

The girls were scared. They started talking super fast, and telling me, "Go! Go! Go!"

I made it. I don't think the other motorcycle expected that of me at all. He hadn't sped up to the degree that I had. I crossed the intersection where he would have been, headed over the tiny little bridge, and continued on in frantic desperation to evade my pursuers.

I could see the lights of the motorcycles come together at the bridge. They needed to come up with another plan, now that that one had failed. I knew one good plan was for them to lay in wait for my return. There was no other way out of the village, after all.

The girls started to panic, "Tere (my nickname), you can't go back! They are waiting for you. You must stay!"

I had still been trying to contact my husband, but our cell service still wasn't working. I had no idea how I was going to be able to get a message to him, and you better believe he would start to worry. If I didn't turn up during the next hour, he would know something had happened, especially if he called our other teammates and knew they had returned but I hadn't.

I knew I couldn't go back, but I also knew I needed to get word to my husband. There really was no other road out. So I drove to the first girl's house and dropped her off. I went to the second girl's house, and as I dropped her off, the girl told her mom about what had happened. She offered to let me call my husband on her phone.

She handed me the phone, I dialed, and it rang. Thankfully, Mike picked up. With the biggest sigh of relief, I told him what had happened. He was ready to come out and get me. We only had one car, and I was currently in it. But he was ready to go over to our teammates house and get their car.

I told him, "No way! They are lying in wait. You will just fall into the trap they are setting up for me." And there was no calling the police. This was a community that the police simply won't go into. So there was nothing for it but to wait it out.

One of the girls in our group was from the family that we had spent a lot of time with, so she jumped in with the solution."Tere, you will come to my house and stay."

"Are you SURE?" I asked, knowing that the motorcycle guys might come looking for me.

"YES!" she replied.

In the little center part of the village there was a big soccer field and about six little dead-end roads that fanned out from there. Thankfully, her house was at the end of one of these little roads, away from the main road, so the bad guys wouldn't see my car. And I had turned off headlights so I wouldn't be visible.

When we arrived at my friend's house, we explained what had happened. Without a second thought, she agreed to let me stay. She told me to drive my car into their tiny yard. Then she put a wire across the yard and quickly covered my car with shrubs and bushes. Soon you would never have known that a car was there.

To say I was tired was to be generous. I was exhausted. The adrenaline that had kept me going, helping me make decisions and keep away from my pursuers, was draining out. My friend took me into one of the rooms, tucked me in bed, and shut the little door.

I doubt that any of my readers have slept in a jungle before. I hadn't. I had done plenty of camping growing up, but I must say I had never tried to sleep in a jungle. The humming cicadas, the restless nocturnal animals, the bedbugs and the mosquitos barely let me sleep that night, but I must have slept some because morning came soon enough.

I woke up, bleary-eyed, to a cup of coffee waiting for me. My friend had been up much earlier to start her day. Part of her day was heading into the jungle to collect firewood and getting her wood stove going for the day. She also had to get ready to head to the river to wash the family's clothes. It was a tough life in the jungle.

Sipping my coffee, I pondered the night I had just been through. I wasn't oblivious to the dangers of where I lived. I had heard of missionaries that had been killed in the line of duty. I knew from my nine years of military training that when something bad is going to happen, it's going to happen. All my training wasn't going to help me against two armed men up to no good. But God had preserved me, found me safe shelter, and provided for me. He wasn't done with me yet.

I thanked my friend profusely. She offered to let me stay as long as I wanted, but honestly, I just wanted to get back home, to be there with my husband and feel safe. So, I drank my coffee, kissed her on the cheek, un-camouflaged my car, and headed home.

My cell service was working again, and I got a text on my phone. Unbeknownst to me, Mike had sent out a prayer chain request, and the prayer warriors were hard at work. People were praying for me, and my BFF sent a text from her U.S. phone to my Honduras phone with the perfect scripture, "The name of the Lord is a strong tower. The righteous run to it and are safe." – Proverbs 18:10.

"In peace I will both lie down and sleep; for you alone, O Lord, make me dwell in safety." – Psalm 4:8

Chapter 42

The "Kiss", the Prom and other stories that made me look stupid

"For we are strangers before you and sojourners, as all our fathers were. Our days on the earth are like a shadow, and there is no abiding." – 1 Chronicles 29:15

As a new missionary in a new-to-you country, there are so many cultural things you have to figure out. The language is one thing, but how do you hail a taxi? Where do you go to pay your electric bill? How do you register your kid into school? How do you buy a car, open a bank account, rent a house? We were the first missionaries from our agency to go to Honduras, so we had no one that had "been there, done that" to help us through this process. We had to figure out everything by ourselves, which was no easy feat, I might add. One situation in which we were learning the ropes almost ended our ministry, or so we thought.

At that time in Honduras, public schools only went up to sixth grade. So, graduation from sixth grade was as big a deal as high school graduation in the States. Families gathered from all parts of the country, big feasts were organized, and the graduation ceremony was extravagant. During the ceremony, the graduate has a representative present them and has a special dance with them. To be asked to be this person is considered a high honor. Our first year in Honduras, Mike was asked to be this person for one of the families we had come to know and love dearly.

One of the things the representative does is get a special gift for the graduate. Instead of risking getting something the graduate wouldn't want, Mike decided to take the young lady and her mother out for a shopping day to buy her a new outfit. As they waited in a shop to be helped, the young woman looked over at Mike and kissed in his direction. Mike was stunned. He didn't know what to do. She looked at him again, pursed her lips, and kissed in his direction again. He knew it was over. He knew our ministry was done—we would have to leave the country—here was a young girl picking up on him! He was devastated.

Finally, in exasperation, the young woman said, "Look, Miguel, another Miguel," and pursed her lips again. Mike looked to his left and saw that he was sitting next to a mirror. Now he understood! She was "lip pointing," something that is very common in Honduras. To point with your finger is considered very rude, so you point with your lips. But to an American, it looked like he was being kissed at.

Whew! Crisis averted!

We were learning. Slowly but surely, we were figuring out the different phrases, different foods, and different traditions that made up Honduran culture. By the end of seven years, you would think we would have had most things figured out, but there were still hurdles to be crossed. As a missionary, you go to a foreign country to serve, but the other part of being a missionary is just living life. You have to learn new ways to cook, to clean, to send mail, and to be part of cultural events like soccer matches. For our daughter, that meant experiencing prom.

High school senior prom. Yes, they even have prom in Honduras. It's a huge event. There were committees formed, meetings for parents held, and tickets purchased. We were shocked at how much the prom cost, but we didn't want Madison to miss the prom, nor the cultural experience. About a month before the event, we were given the prom invitation and ten tickets.

Ten tickets? What in the world? Why would Madison need TEN tickets? What about her date, and dinner, and all that stuff? In

Honduras, the prom is not a date function; it is a family function. The ten tickets were for the prom attendee and nine of her family members. Well, that's different! But Madison didn't have nine family members to invite, nor did she want to invite any friends. So, we put the extra tickets up for sale and had at least four families pounce. I couldn't possibly imagine that now one family was going to have sixteen people in attendance! I just couldn't fathom it.

With the extra tickets sold, next came the dress. There was really only one store in town that sold prom-style dresses. We went to this store and looked around. Madison was not impressed by anything there. Hondurans like bling—they like it a LOT. All the dresses we found had bling and lots of it. That was just not Madison's style. Not at all. I was thrilled she was actually going to wear a dress. She is a pants, shorts, sweatshirt kind of girl. But she agreed to a dress, and she wanted to design it. A lot of clothing in Honduras is tailor-made, and many other girls were having their dresses fitted to their size and style as well.

We headed out to the local fabric store, and Madison picked out her fabric. She had a dress design she had found online, and we took the fabric and a picture of the dress to a local seamstress. Thankfully we went in plenty of time because everyone in the shop was working overtime to finish dresses for a number of local proms coming up.

A few weeks later, we had the dress in hand. We then went to our hair dresser and set up the date and time for her up-do, emphasizing to her the importance of timeliness for the big event. She understood, and we felt confident everything was falling into place.

Prom morning arrived. We went to the hair dresser, but when she saw us, her face dropped. She was right in the middle of three different clients who were all in various stages of coloring and other time-consuming matters. She knew she had messed up. There was simply not going to be enough time for us. We sat for an hour, hoping she would be able to squeeze us in, but it wasn't going to happen. So we left. Now it was up to me. Oh my goodness. I have braided and styled Madison's hair her entire life. But for a prom?! My heart started to pound.

We went home, and Madison said, "Mom, whatever you do, it's going to be great!"

I looked online for some tutorials on elegant hair styles, and then went to work. About an hour later I came up with a style that looked really becoming on my girl. Whew! I was satisfied.

We all got dressed and left the house at 6:45, not wanting to be late. When we arrived, we were the first people there. They were still setting up! You would think after seven years we would have figured out that the time listed on any announcement was the time to start getting ready, not the actual time for the event to start. But we were there, so we stayed.

We got to our assigned table and sat and waited. Slowly, a few families started filtering in. And then I knew I was in trouble. Boxes and boxes of decorations, food, plate settings, candles, champagne, etc. were being pulled out by each family: they were setting up their own tables. If you have known me long enough, you will know that I really don't care about this kind of thing. But Mike and I both knew that we had to fix this, and fast! We did not want to be ones sticking out of the crowd any more than we already were. Mike looked at me, and he took off. The closest store was closed, but there was a gas station nearby that sold stuff as well. About an hour later he returned. He pulled out a box of crackers, packaged cheese chunks, sliced salami, soda and paper plates, and we quickly set up our table as best we could. Man, were we out of our element!

While he had been gone, my angst got even deeper. When I looked at the other women coming in, I knew I was way, way, way underdressed. I truly had on what was best in my closet, but as a missionary working in a village with very poor people, there simply wasn't any reason to have a really nice dress. I had never had any occasion in the seven years we had been there to wear one. But the moms and aunts at the prom all had amazing dresses on: some looked like wedding dresses, others looked like gowns for the most expensive gala you can imagine. But there was no changing it, so what could I do?

Munching on peanuts and salami, we waited for the thing to start. They gathered all the prom attendees and escorted them out of the room. It was time for the presentation of the students, but we had no idea what to do. Thankfully, it was alphabetical, and having a last name that started with "P" gave us an opportunity to observe. Each young man was escorted in by his mother, with his father behind them, while a statement about that student was read aloud. Each young woman was escorted by her father, and her mother was behind the couple. The couple was paraded around the room in a circle and then joined those already presented to form a larger circle. Now knowing what to do, Mike and I ran back to Madison. We entered, presented her to the crowd, and took our place in the big circle.

Then the actual festivities commenced. As there were no dates, everyone danced with everyone—parents danced with kids, friends danced with friends. Multiple formal pictures were taken. It was actually a lot of fun! It was a different, yet really neat way to have a prom. For many of these young people who would begin working upon graduation, this was the last chance for them to live the life of a kid.

Mike and I wanted to be dutiful parents, so we were not going to bail until Madison was good and ready. By 10:30, my non-partying, introverted kid was ready to go, but it was then that dinner started to be served. Wow, 10:30 at night?! We had paid a lot for our tickets, so we decided to stay. It took a good thirty minutes to pass out plates to the nearly 500 people in attendance. We ate our shrimp and other delicious food, and Madison made the rounds to say good-bye. It was then that people realized what we were doing. And the looks we got were ones we won't forget! It was as if every face in the entire room looked our way. I had my purse in hand, Madison had her shoes in her hand, and we were headed toward the door.

At 11:30 p.m., we were the first to leave. People couldn't believe it. We were pretty sure we could hear in their minds, "Oh, that poor little gringo family. They just don't know better, do they?" Off we went, and the party went on, and on, and on. I have no idea what time it actually ended.

Just living life in another country can bring with it all sorts of stressors, faux paus, and examples of us showing our own stupidity. Another case in point:

There was a family in the village that had kind of adopted us since our arrival in country. They had helped us get through some cultural challenges (the "kiss" story above—yeah, that was them). We often went to their house to just hang out. She taught me how to make tortillas. I had helped treat her dying mother in their house. We all had bonded.

On one such occasion we were at their house and I had my camera with me. It had occurred to me that I really didn't have any good pictures of them as a family. The mom and her two eldest daughters, who were twenty-four and twenty-one, posed for me to take a photo. In the Honduras heat, attire is as uncovered as possible. Women typically wear flip flops, skirts, and short shirts. Why do I mention this? Well, the three women in front of me were wearing what I would consider fairly revealing tops. They stood together, turned a little sideways, put their hands on their hips, and smiled mischievously. They were having fun. So I tried to have fun back with them. Since the three ladies standing all "sexy" were moms, I said to them, "Que mámas!" And they giggled, then laughed, and got even more into the picture.

Mike leaned over to me and said,"Watch your accent! It's 'Que mamás!' Not 'Que mámas!'"

There aren't a lot of words in Spanish where accent is important, but there are a few, and those few are VERY important. My face went bright red. What I meant to say was, "Wow! What moms!" Instead I said, "Wow! What breasts!"

All I can say is I'm glad they know and love us well. I think they were actually flattered because they kept up their shenanigans. I don't think they really knew that I had made a mistake. But that stayed with me for a very long time, and you better believe my husband has never let me live that one down!

"So then you are no longer strangers and aliens, but you are fellow citizens with the saints and members of the household of God," - Ephesians 2:19

Chapter 43

Struggle

"A hot-tempered person stirs up conflict, but the one who is patient calms a quarrel" (Proverbs 15:18).

Let's be perfectly clear: I am a sinner. You are a sinner. We have come to work in a country filled with sinners. It's what we are and what we do. I include myself in that because I know it and see it in myself all the time. Every day is a struggle to be godly, to act in a godly way, and to let others know we are different. I know that I often don't do things the right way. I speak before I think. I am a passionate person and fight for what I believe to be right. I have trampled people on my way to accomplish those things.

Through every situation, I try to learn something—a better way to handle conflict, a better way to love my enemy, a better way to assess my faults. So, I bring to you some stories of conflict, filled with hurt and anger. Filled with fault all around. I don't bring them saying I am without fault; I simply bring them to allow us an opportunity to learn from them.

"For all have sinned and fall short of the glory of God." - Romans 3:23

"Why do you see the speck that is in your brother's eye, but do not notice the log that is in your own eye?" -Matthew 7:3)

"For by works of the law no human being will be justified in his sight, since through the law comes knowledge of sin." - Romans 3:20

"but God shows his love for us in that while we were still sinners, Christ died for us." -Romans 5:8

A friend of mine, who is not a full-time missionary but has observed team conflict on short-term mission trips, said, "Erin, team conflict on the mission field seems to be everyone's dirty little secret, and it shouldn't be."

She was right. It's learning while you are in that conflict that is important. It's learning how to work with a body of believers that you may not even like, but with whom you share a common purpose. You learn how to be gracious in the middle of chaos. You learn how to hear and you work to be heard. Conflict is a part of life, and being a part of mission life is no different.

Each person on a team comes to the field with their own life experiences, their own story, and their own baggage. When Mike and I started with our mission agency and went to Honduras, we knew we were going to be the "odd man out," if you will. During the majority of our training we were by far the oldest couple, with the oldest child, and because of that, the most life experience. Mike was typically the only guy around without a Masters of Divinity, and I was typically the only married woman who was a full-time mom, a full-time missionary, and employed full-time as well. On top of that, we were from California, another rare and odd fact in the mission world.

As women, we come with our own baggage as well. We spend an exorbitant amount of time comparing ourselves to our peers and comparing our children to other women's children. I've noticed it with every facet of life—a woman's battle cry is how long she was in labor, or how easily she became pregnant. We wear all of these "badges" and compare ourselves with those around us. I don't know why, but it's what we do. Is this right? No, of course it isn't, but this is the dichotomy of the flesh and the heart. Our heart knows what is right, but we are betrayed by our flesh.

"Watch and pray that you may not enter into temptation. The spirit indeed is willing, but the flesh is weak." -Matthew 26:41.

During our training, one of the things that was discussed was that we take to the field the same things we have in the States. I'm not talking about physical things. We take our idiosyncrasies, we take our rough edges, we take our talents, but we also take our issues. These issues that we can easily hide or deal with in the comfort of what we know become compounded when we enter cultures that we don't know. What was a small issue become humongous when we hit the mission field. What were annoying habits in the States become the center for conflict. It's like being on the mission field brings out not only the best in us, but it also highlights the worst. When everything about living becomes stressful—buying groceries, paying bills, enrolling your child in school, buying a car, knowing where to put your trash—then everything else is compounded as well. The rough edges simply are more noticeable. Everything becomes magnified.

God is sanctifying us. He is the potter, and we are the clay. Sometimes that clay needs to be pounded down, refined, and the edges smoothed out. Sanctification will mean being put into circumstances that are uncomfortable, that point us toward God, and away from ourselves. Because how can we get through these times relying simply upon ourselves? We can't.

When you go on a construction site there are warning signs all around. Businesses are required to post hazard signs and Material Safety Data Sheets. So wouldn't it be great if we all had our own "warning signs" hanging around our neck? "Warning: explodes when stressed." "Warning: toxic person ahead." "Keep off the path. Conflict ahead." In a sense, we do. Warning signs are there if you know what to look for.

Think about your time at your job. Are you friends with everyone there? No. Is there struggle and strife in your job? Conflict between management and employees? As a nurse manager I was required to go to seminars every year, and typically there was at least one breakout session that talked about conflict. Because the reality is, it's not if but when it is going to happen, and you need to know how to deal with it.

The church is no different. A number of the churches we know and love have even been through church splits because of conflict or difference in direction. And God knew that His people would fight, they would bicker, and He gave us guidance in the Bible that speaks directly to this. Just because we are people of God does not leave us immune to our own sin, the sins of others, and weaknesses of the flesh.

Conflict is a fact of life in business and the church. So why does it come as a shock or surprise when there are the same kinds of problems on the mission field? My husband wrote a blog entitled, "Missionary, liar, liar, pants on fire." In it, he addresses the difficulty missionaries face in being transparent about their struggles when they speak in front of churches or post on blogs or in newsletters. We hear about cars that break down and medical issues that crop up, but not about a mother crying over her child, convinced she has done the worst thing by taking her child away from everything in the U.S. to a Third World country. (That was me, by the way.) We never hear a man talk about the struggle he faces to ensure that his family is spiritually fed, that his prayer life should be better, than he often dreads going and doing ministry that day because he just doesn't have it in him.

And why is that? We have, for some reason, this adversarial relationship with our supporters. We need to portray ourselves as being well and healthy, having everything in order. If not, churches or individuals may stop supporting us, and we can't be on the field without it. So, we hide. We hide the trials. We hide the tribulation. We hide the struggles.

It got to a point in my life I couldn't hide it anymore. So, I wrote a blog, and it was transparent. I wrote of my struggles, my internal pain. And guess what? I got more personal e-mails, private messages, and even cards in the mail offering encouragement, prayer, support, and most of all—love. Love. I was loved. It didn't matter that I was broken and having issues. And so, almost without exception, whenever we choose to be transparent with our struggles, those blog posts get way more traffic than our other "here's what's happening" blog posts.

Not only do individuals struggle, but teams struggle as well. We had a couple that came to visit on a vision trip to consider our location as a new ministry site for them. The wife asked me who on the team was my best friend. When I told her my best friend was not someone on the team, she was startled. I was the oldest woman on the team. I had a teenage daughter. And I had my own ministry. No one else on the team could relate. Most of the other missionary women had children in diapers or kindergarten. We walked different paths and were in different seasons of life. I was totally distracted when I sat with them in their kitchens to talk, with children crying, pulling on their clothes, making messes, and getting into mischief. I hadn't been in a household of little children in a long, long time. It just wasn't me. And because of that, there was an automatic wall that seemed to surround me.

We go onto the field understanding that we face the challenge of learning and understanding a new language and a new culture. However, what we don't anticipate are the cultural differences within our own team. You would think that as North Americans we would at least have a basic understanding of a similar culture, but I'm here to tell you differently. When you think of a Californian, what do you think of? Loud, tells it the way it is, tattoos, and unafraid of confrontation. Yes, I fit every one of those categories. Imagine that culture going into a Midwestern or Southern culture. It's a recipe for disaster, and one we never saw coming.

The first time I had anger directed at me from a teammate, I was totally perplexed and completely caught off guard. My way of working through a problem is to hit it head on. I'm not a hide-things-under-the-rug kind of person, nor am I a nitpicker of non-issues. If I have a problem that needs addressing, I address it. What I need to work on sometimes, is in how I do that. I don't like things to fester, so oftentimes I want to address a problem when it occurs.

But many people, such as the people I was working with, don't function that way. And unbeknownst to me, this particular issue had been on this person's mind for the last two years, but she had never talked to me about it, until she was ready to explode.

"15If your brother sins against you, go and tell him his fault, between you and him alone. If he listens to you, you have gained your brother. 16But if he does not listen, take one or two others along with you, that every charge may be established by the evidence of two or three witnesses. 17If he refuses to listen to them, tell it to the church." (Matthew 18:15-17).

I was notified that there was going to be a meeting. What I didn't know was that I was the reason for the meeting. I found myself sitting in a room of people, including a visiting pastor and my teammates. The meeting started with a roundtable discussion to "get everything out on the table." I listened and my face crumpled as I began to understand. They were mad at me. They didn't like how I dealt with things. It grated on their nerves. And this was the platform they were going to use to let me know.

Now it was my turn to speak my mind. I was in tears. I was in shock. I stood up and told them, "I feel betrayed. You have been sitting on this anger and frustration for two years and never said anything about it. You never gave me an opportunity to alter how I did things or to allow me a chance to speak about it. Instead, I find myself hearing about it for the first time here as it is talked about in a room full of people."

The room was silent. Understanding dawned on their faces. They hadn't considered my perspective.

And now I was angry and hurt. Where were the steps of biblical reconciliation? I don't remember having been talked to one-on-one, and certainly not approached by two people. I suddenly found myself in front of a firing squad, unequipped and unprepared.

Reconciliation came as we started to understand the culture of our team and the culture of individuals within our team. We realized that we had not approached this whole thing the right way. We were figuring out what conflict was and how to work through it. We learned that we each had to give a little. I needed to come to the middle, as did they. We understood that we loved each other as brothers and sisters in Christ, but that didn't necessarily mean we were going to all get along. And I began to understand that even more difficult than learning our host culture was learning to work with our own team culture.

As new teammates came on and off the field, the norms were constantly changing. The personalities, seasons of life, and personal expectations they brought with them brought up more issues. I was once again the target of a teammate's anger. Instead of letting the situation boil up, I took this person out for breakfast. It was then it all came out: "I can't be you. I can't be what you are. I can't be what you expect of me."

I looked at her and said, "What do you think I expect of you? And what do you think I am?"

She replied, "You are everything—a mom and a wife with a full-time ministry, and you expect that same of me."

My eyebrows furrowed as I tried to understand where she was coming from. I finally told her, "My only expectation for you is the expectation for you to be what you want to be. If that means a mom and a wife, then be a good mom and a good wife. If you want to have your own ministry, then be good at what you do. I have no expectations other than that."

The relief was evident on her face. She was trying to live up to what she had decided were my expectations of her. In the end, she was a great wife and a great mom, and we weren't the best of friends. We never really hung-out. We didn't watch movies at each other's house. And we had more misunderstandings and conflicts in the future, but that was okay. Learning to do conflict right is what is important

I wrote a blog post on maintaining traditions. In it I talked about how important it is to my family that we maintain our traditions no matter what country we were in. One of our other traditions is celebrating the Fourth of July. I asked Mike to never organize short-term teams to be in country during this week. I am patriotic to a fault. I have always had a U.S. flag in my home, and I fly it on all the appropriate holidays. I cry at the beginning of ball games when the National Anthem is sung. It's important to me, and I want my daughter to have an understanding of her heritage.

But this blog prompted a response I hadn't anticipated. Someone commented on the post, and I could tell that it had bothered them. So, I went back to my blog to figure out what about it was bothering them. I had written about my observation that Missionary Kids can sometimes lose part of their U.S. heritage. They are being educated in a foreign country, and that country isn't going to focus on U.S. history—our national anthem and the Pledge of Allegiance, the Founding Fathers, the Magna Carta—that kind of thing. I had stated that I felt it was my job to teach my kid about that because it was important to me.

When I realized my post might have been misunderstood—that the reader may have thought I meant that all families should have the same priorities I did—I went back and edited the post to make my statements more generalized.

Later in the day, another unpleasant comment appeared on my post. I sent the commenter a private message, trying to find out what was the source of the problem. Then the anger that had been pent up for a long time, that I knew nothing about, came pouring out. I was accused of slander. I was accused of not pursuing reconciliation. I was accused of not hearing her. I was accused of things that had nothing to do with my blog. I was dumbfounded. I was hurt. What was happening?!

This person started bringing up things that she wasn't even involved in. This meant that private conversations had occurred about these incidents. I was accused of refusing to reconcile with individuals after several attempts. This confused me, so I spoke up. "I have not received a single message from anyone. How have there been attempts of reconciliation if no one has contacted me? That doesn't make any sense."

In the end, the friendship was severed. I never heard from that person again.

I sat in a room full of women at an island dive center who had gathered for a weekend of spiritual renewal. This was an annual event, a time to come together and learn from our leaders, reflect on our time with God, pray, and have fun. The location and the format were chosen a year in advance. We had brought in two speakers who had spent a lot of time and raised a lot of money to prepare a special time for us. As we left the introductory lesson, I looked forward to the rest of the weekend with excitement.

About twenty minutes later I got a knock at my door. All of the other women, including the speakers, filed into my room and stood opposite me. They wanted to talk about the schedule—they were disappointed that there wasn't more time allotted for snorkeling and diving. I reminded them that the schedule had been planned for over a year and that they could have spoken up about changes to it earlier. Our speakers had prepared their lessons based on that schedule and it wouldn't be fair to them to change it now.

The backlash hit hard and fast. *You aren't hearing me. You aren't feeling my heart. You don't care about me. What's wrong with you? Why are you so difficult?* And on and on it went, attack after attack after attack. The speakers looked at me, at a loss for what to do.

The next day we all met back in our main room, and the speakers agreed to rearrange the schedule so that the people who wanted to do the afternoon dive could do so. But this meant that our last session of the day was going to be at 9 p.m. So, after a long day, we were going to try and be spiritually edified while we were all exhausted. I shook my head. This really was not a good option. But everyone else agreed, and so it was set.

I waited for people to come find me and try to reconcile the situation. I was hoping that people would have prayed and realized that even though they had disagreed with me, the way that it was handled was not right. I kept waiting, but no one came.

I knew I couldn't let this sit. So, I approached the first person and told her I really wanted to get together and talk about what happened.

She said she would think about it. I approached the second and received the same response. I approached the third, whose response was "Absolutely not." The fourth person I approached agreed to meet with me.

After I had been attacked, I was reaching out and working for reconciliation. As no one was searching me out, I would search them out. And one by one, we met. Ultimately, we didn't agree about what had transpired, but we at least came to an understanding, with the exception of one individual. This person continued to refuse to talk to me. I approached her the next day, but she continued to refuse my attempts to talk. That night during our nine o'clock session, I looked around the room, and two people had fallen asleep during the session. They were tired as it had been a long day. It was not a good time to attempt to learn and grow spiritually, just as I had feared.

The following day the last individual finally agreed to meet with me. Words were exchanged, but nothing really of substance was said. I felt like this was left unfinished, but it was made very clear that the conversation was at an end. Just because we were Christians didn't mean we were always going to do it right.

> *⁷Submit yourselves therefore to God. Resist the devil, and he will flee from you. ⁸Draw near to God, and he will draw near to you. Cleanse your hands, you sinners, and purify your hearts, you double-minded.⁹Be wretched and mourn and weep. Let your laughter be turned to mourning and your joy to gloom. Humble yourselves before the Lord, and he will exalt you" (James 4:7-10).*

The Bible is great when addressing the issue of conflict. Throughout the scriptures you can find people and groups in conflict, and God speaks so wisely of ways to work through it. There are many books written on conflict resolution. Most mission agencies have counselors. In addition, many mission organizations offer courses and training on how to work through this. So why write this?

First, I write this to get the dirty little secret out there. If you are a missionary on a team that has conflict and you are the primary source causing the conflict—be convicted! You may not even realize that you are the primary source for that conflict. However, even if you are only ten percent responsible for the conflict, you are one hundred percent responsible for your ten percent. Search your heart and seek help. Find help within your mission agency or supporting churches.

> *"What causes quarrels and what causes fights among you? Is it not this, that your passions are at war within you? You desire and do not have, so you murder. [2]You covet and cannot obtain, so you fight and quarrel. You do not have, because you do not ask. [3]You ask and do not receive, because you ask wrongly, to spend it on your passions" -James 4:1-3*

Second, if you are on the other side of the conflict, you also must be convicted. Be convicted to seek out guidance in how to be part of the solution. I want you, as a person on a team, to know you aren't alone. You aren't alone in struggling through conflict on a team. You may feel too afraid to tell someone because you feel like you are alone. But the secret is out! I may even be so bold as to say that conflict is not the exception on missions teams, it is the norm. Missionaries are on the front lines. Satan has limited resources, and he is not going to waste his time on those who aren't out there trying to make a difference. Those on "God's team" need to be vigilant, pray, and be proactive. More teams than you know of are dealing with conflict issues, just as you are.

Third, if you are someone interested in missions, then understand that this is real. That it's typically not if, but when, conflict will happen. Be proactive to seek out ways to equip yourself and understand good biblical principles for working through team conflict. And then don't just hear it, apply it. But go into missions with an understanding that we are all sinners. You are a sinner, your teammates are sinners, and those we go to serve are sinners. And there will be conflict. Don't go in unaware and get blindsided. Go in equipped and prepared.

Finally, if you are a supporter of missionaries, if you are on a missions committee, or if you are a leader in the church, know that the odds are your missionaries are struggling through some of these issues. They may feel like they can't say some of these things because of the adversarial relationship that many feel they have. So seek them out and ask probing questions. *What are your biggest personal struggles right now?* This may give them "permission" to feel like they can speak their minds.

Teams have both triumphed and failed because of team conflict. So let's not keep this our "dirty little secret" any more. It's a reality.

> *"³¹Let all bitterness and wrath and anger and clamor and slander be put away from you, along with all malice. ³²Be kind to one another, tenderhearted, forgiving one another, as God in Christ forgave you" (Ephesians 4:31-32).*

Chapter 44

Reflections on my Time in Honduras

Our time in Honduras was one filled with hardships and joy, challenges and overcoming obstacles. We were especially challenged as we had to figure out everything by ourselves. But God saw fit to use us to accomplish His work. What had become my life, I realize, looks different to those who don't live there.

Armenia Bonito was the community we worked in. These are some of the things we observed there:

When someone was diagnosed with cancer it was a death sentence; hardly anyone could afford the treatment, no matter what type of cancer they had.

A compound fracture was poorly repaired, or just amputated because it was cheaper.

Childbirth was lonely, scary, and oftentimes dangerous. Obstetric emergencies almost always led to death.

Just preparing and eating a meal took enormous time and effort. They had to collect wood in the jungle to make their fire to cook their food, while we turn a switch to cook ours.

Women trekked down to the river with their laundry where they scrubbed their clothes on a wash rack or on a rock in the river, then trekked back to their house and hung them on a line. We throw our clothes in a machine, flick a switch and get out fresh, clean laundry in an hour.

Women cried in desperation over their severely sick children, wondering if they would survive to see the next day, while we are allowed to sleep in a sleep chair in an air-conditioned hospital room where nurses and doctors care for our little ones.

We get grumpy because we have to buy school supplies for our children when they enter school. Families in Honduras can't even send their children to school because they can't buy the simple pencil they need to attend.

In the U.S., we receive food stamps to sustain us if we are in dire straights. In Honduras, people die on the streets from starvation because there are no social services to help them out.

There are many nine-year-old girls who never have the chance to be children because they are too busy caring for their younger siblings. And in the U.S. we have children who complain because they have to wash the dishes.

So, what did we, as missionaries who served in this beautiful country, see?

Children laughing and playing, just grateful to be alive. Women who lived every day to be a role model to their children and gave up everything to put food on the table. We saw people who were craving to know the God who is our Heavenly Father. We saw people who knew their lives would be harsh and short, but they lived for the moment! We saw people who loved their elderly and cared for them, not as a burden, but as a joy.

Oh, how we can learn from these amazing, resilient people! How I love to give the love that God has given to me. But I also learned to love life like those in Honduras. What a blessing indeed to have lived in and among these amazing people.

Chapter 45

Leaving How I started – With One Box

"For we are his workmanship, created in Christ Jesus for good works, which God prepared beforehand, that we should walk in them." – Ephesians 2:10

Seven and a half years ago, the very first medical event I put on by myself was a pregnancy medical clinic. I had taught childbirth classes for more than twenty years in the States, and felt that I was equipped to be able to do this. I took blood pressure, checked blood sugar, measured bellies, handed out prenatal vitamins, and even sent a mom to the hospital to have her baby (see Chapter 6: The Baby). Before we had a car, we rode an hour and a half each way on the bus to Armenia Bonito, the little village of 3,000 we served in. That is how the humble beginnings of our ministry started.

Now we have a permanent clinic hosted by an incredible Honduran physician, Dr. Roger, and an amazing Honduran nurse. We have treated more than 4,000 patients a year, and host two or three medical brigades a year.

About a week before we were to leave Honduras for good, I went out to the clinic. Part of my responsibility over the years had been ensuring we had sufficient supplies and medication to help the patients we saw. This included applying for grants, putting on supply and over the counter medication drives at churches, asking for baby clothing, etc. It also included organizing medical brigades to come and bringing medication to help the clinic see to the needs of those we served. I've collected laboratory supplies including a high-end microscope, four exam beds, and more equipment and medical supplies than will probably ever be used in the lifetime of the clinic. I started collecting medical supplies before I even left the States. Hospitals donated expired exam gloves, sutures, etc. We had these shipped to Honduras, and that was how I started the clinic.

Now I was headed off to a new country to start a new ministry. Once again I was going to be starting a medical/ mercy ministry from scratch, all on my own. I went to the clinic that I had quite literally shed blood, sweat and tears over, and looked around. It was amazing. It was incredible what God had created in the time we were here. We had a clinic in the jungle, serving the poorest of the poor. We could check people for urinary tract infections, pregnancies, malaria, dengue, and other illnesses. We had a fully stocked pharmacy (better than the public hospital's, I might add) and supplies that our doctor hadn't even seen, including a neo-natal ambu-bag and IV start kits. We could take care of emergencies, if need be, with emergency medication and IV solutions. We had pulse oximeters, nebulizers, oxygen tanks; it was a full-on medical clinic. I took it all in. I had accomplished what I had come to do, and God had provided everything to make it happen.

So, I looked around and wondered what I should take with me to start my new ministry. Going to this little country in Africa, where the healthcare was significantly worse than Honduras, I knew that I needed my wits, my education, and my God with me. But what else did I need? I decided to leave with what I had arrived with. I put together in one small box three things—my stethoscope, my otoscope, and my childbirth education material.

Humble beginnings...humble leavings.

And this is how I started my new ministry in Africa—with my little box of medical personal effects. I arrived into Honduras humbly, and I left humbly, to start anew.

When I left the clinic for the last time, I couldn't help but shed a tear. I had come, been obedient to my calling, and met the needs of the community and beyond. I had personally served over 10,000 patients, and the clinic was seeing about 4,000 patients a year. It was humbling. I am just a nurse, after all. It would never have occurred to me while I was in nursing school, or even working at the pediatric hospital, that this was something that I would one day do. God had instilled in me this passion, this burning desire to serve His people where He called me. I'm not an intellectual genius, so I bring to the table the only thing I know: that God will equip me, He will sustain me, and He will be glorified through the work He has me do.

My sweet friend Mindy Hertzell put it this way: "This picture seems just right. At the end of it all you will journey to new places with naught more than you started with once before, and begin again. Daunting? Yes. But with God all things are possible. While it's a little box of supplies, it was your start to countless lives changed; thousands of vitamins given; hours of assessments; medication administration; glasses fitted; teeth cleaned, pulled, and filled; diabetes and htn (hypertension) education; abx (antibiotic) dosing; maternal/newborn checks; counseling; inventory; the building of an actual, functioning, life-giving CLINIC! IN THE JUNGLE! You walked miles to check in on people weekly, sweated buckets under a tin roof during mobile clinic times, provided safety, hugged freely, loved deeply, and above all else introduced each one to the Great Physician who heals our deepest wounds and gives us eternal life. And all you had to start with was that little box of supplies. Seems like a pretty special box to me."

"For it is God who works in you, both to will and to work for his good pleasure." – Philippians 2:13

Chapter 46

Deep Loss

"Honor your father and your mother, as the Lord your God commanded you, that your days may be long, and that it may go well with you in the land that the Lord your God is giving you." – Deuteronomy 5:16

One of the things you give up when you follow the calling of God to the mission field is the closeness of friends and family. That's not to say they're no longer there, but the easy phone calls, the trips to go visit during the holidays, the barbecues at dear friends' houses, and the girls' nights out are gone. They just are. It is a reality that some people have a hard time with. We've had missionaries that had come to join us that ended up leaving the field because to be without that support net underneath them was simply more than they could stand.

It is also interesting the friendships you develop on the field. We had a family that came to Honduras on a vision trip to see if Honduras would be the site of their future ministry. One of the questions that the ladies on the trip asked me was who my best friend was. She honestly was shocked when I told her that my dearest and sweetest friends were back in the States. She was waiting for me to tell her which of the women on the field were my best friends, and when it wasn't any of them, this really surprised her.

You see, we are a group of people all thrown together by God, to work for His Glory and for His Kingdom. But that doesn't mean we are here to be best friends. I asked this visiting woman if she was BFFs with all the women at her church, to which her quick and immediate response was NO!

So I said, "Why would it be any different here?"

The ladies on my team were all in different stages of life than I was. They didn't know my baggage, they didn't know my likes and dislikes. They didn't know what makes me tick. I am well past the stage of diapers, babies, and preteens. I had a full life before missions. Most of the other women had not had jobs before they arrived on the mission field, so we were coming from very different places in life. This was not a bad thing, it was just a thing.

So, there is a sense of being alone on the mission field, even though you are in a large group of people. This also holds true if your paths lead in a very different direction. All the ladies on our team had little kiddos, so they were very limited in the time they spent outside of their families. Again, it was not a bad thing. But I was a full-time wife, a full-time mom, and a full-time missionary. I started, developed, and created a full mobile medical clinic and a full-time permanent clinic. I ran all the medical brigades that came through and hired a physician and a nurse to work with me. My life, work, and mission experience was very different than most of the people on my team.

For the last ten years my mother had been in a declining state of health back home. My dad called me one night and said, "You need to come."

So I went. My mother was in the hospital. She had thrown a clot to her lungs and was in deep respiratory distress. She had so many other physical ailments along with that, this was just one other thing that threw her body into an eventual state of no return. I stayed in the States for two weeks until it appeared she had stabilized. This would happen two more times. When I had returned to Honduras after the third trip, my dad called to tell me that my sweet mother had passed away.

Going through something like this when you are not with your extended family or your church family is one of the most emotionally difficult things I've ever gone through. The grieving was profound. My dad, at the time, was not a believer, and so didn't want to have any type of funeral. There was no closure for me.

Within a year of my mom's passing, my dad became a believer. He became an active member of his church, was involved in every Bible study they offered, attended Bible Study Fellowship, and immersed himself in his new church family. He said that I was the reason for his conversion, but I was only one small brick in the many bricks of believers that had been brought before my dad. The pastor at his church pursued him like I've never seen anyone do before.

For this I was grateful, because right before our departure to Africa, I got the awful phone call from my brother. My father had passed. Unexpected, unexplainable—a heart attack, they think. The reality is, I still don't know, and honestly, it doesn't really matter. He is gone, but not lost. He passed as a believer.

I flew to California to be with my stepsisters and to try and close out the house I had called home for eighteen years of my life. I called up my dad's pastor and pleaded with him to try and get a memorial of some sort together in the few days that all of us were going to be together, and of course he did. While we were cleaning out my dad's house, what did my husband find? My mother's ashes. She had been cremated, and my dad had planned on spreading her ashes around the different places in California that they had travelled in the years they had been married, but he never got around to it. So, my husband and I took her ashes, went to a beautiful lake surrounded by trees and poured what was left of my sweet mother into the waters of that lake. An hour after that, we went to my dad's memorial. The house where the memorial was held was packed. Standing room only. I could only shake my head in complete amazement!

Not even four years before, if my dad had passed away, there would have been no memorial. There wouldn't have been anyone who would have come. But here was his family—his church family—and they couldn't stop talking about what a presence he had been at church. My heart was full and empty at the same time.

What does it mean to lose someone? You can really only understand if you have lost someone who is important to you. It is the price we pay for this great gift of love. Here are the words that this grieving daughter wrote about her father:

How in the world do you start writing down the memories you have of a person who embodied all that it was to be your father? How is it possible to even put into words the reflection of a mourning child who still doesn't comprehend that her father is gone? I guess you just have to start…

An amazing man, a fierce believer in God, a lover of the gospels, a role model, a caretaker, husband to my mother, a fighter…my father.

A man who grew up in a small town in Washington, and moved to the "big city" in California to pursue his dream. He didn't love the outdoors, but made sure that his kids had the experience of hiking and camping, river rafting and snow skiing. He was a man who always put others ahead of himself. My dad taught me through his actions what it meant to be an amazing husband and an incredible father.

I remember one year we were on a weeklong trip of skiing in Bend, Oregon. My parents pulled us out of school, and on the first run of day one, we went to the big slope. No messing around with the little ones—we started way at the tip-top of the mountain. My siblings went first, my mom, then my dad, then me. Well, I hit some powder snow and tried to turn. My body turned, but my skis didn't. I must have made a spectacular fall, as I was immediately surrounded by a whole lot of people, and people were already calling out for the ski patrol to come. In the meantime, my dad had skied quite a ways down, but something stopped him and caused him to look back up. Way up on the hill he saw the commotion of people, but his daughter was nowhere in sight. He knew what that meant. He removed his skis, planted them in the snow, and started to hike back up to where I was. I was immobile, unable to stand up, my ankle shattered. He looked at me, his ever-so-clumsy child, and just hugged me, smiled, and said, "It's all good."

I immediately felt reassured and knew that it was going to be okay. After surgery and an overnight stay in the hospital, I spent the rest of the trip in the ski lodge with a cast on my leg, while the rest of the family enjoyed the weeklong vacation.

My parents would never say that they were nerdy, but that's just what kind of family we were. We were the ones who dressed up to go to the Renaissance Faire, who got pulled out of school and slept overnight in the parking lot of the movie theater so we could be first in to see the latest new release of some cool movie. We transformed our entire house during Halloween into the local haunted house, and my dad always dressed up as Igor and answered the door in his mask, his back hunched, scaring half the kids that came to the door. We played Dungeons and Dragons, and drove forever in our van that had hand-painted peace signs and doves on the outside, while singing songs on our journey and telling jokes to pass the time.

My mother passed away after more than a decade of being sick. While she was sick I would come see them whenever I could, and we fought the fight together as a family. During that time my dad would see my little family coming together with the Lord and praying over my mother. When my mother passed away, he was lost. My heart told me he was going to be one of those guys who, after losing a dear loved one, loses the will to live on. I just knew that he would die in his big house with no one the wiser. He was so quiet and sad, and sat for days endlessly in his home by himself. We contacted Pastor Bob when my mother passed away, and he started reaching out to my dad. He pursued him: he brought comfort, the love of God, and peace to my dad. Soon after, my dad became a believer—just four short months after losing my mom. He jumped into Bible study, joined Bible Study Fellowship, and became active in the church. It was amazing to see the transformation that came over him. My heart rejoiced, and whenever I told the story to anyone, there was no containing my tears of joy.

So here I sit, as a believer, in the quandary of one who lives equally in the midst of extreme sorrow and great joy. The cost of loving deeply is the bottomless sorrow we feel when that person is gone, but it is a price we all pay if we choose to live and love well. The great joy comes in knowing that my dad left this world behind, but woke up in the presence of the almighty God, and I will see him again one day.

My dad credited me with showing him who God is by being a believer, a follower, and a missionary for God. But the reality is that God is clearly there—everywhere—if one only has the eyes to see. God opened my dad's eyes, and took him as His own.

So now how do I finish these memories How do you know you have done your father justice in the retelling of a little of his life? I guess you just do. I will say that I miss him dearly, that I can barely process the fact that he is gone. That I will love him forever.

I wrote these things and share them with you so you can get a glimpse into what made me me. How God has crafted this broken vessel to serve Him.

I went off to Africa, just a few weeks later, now an orphan. My tiny little family got even tinier. That is part of what it is to be a missionary—to be willing to give up the beauty that God has given us with friends and family. I seek to be obedient in what He tells me to do, but it certainly isn't without cost. And this I know. But I long, oh I long to hear the words come out of my Savior's mouth when I have run my race and He is done with me, when I enter into His presence—to hear these words: "Well done, my good and faithful servant."

He will wipe away every tear from their eyes, and death shall be no more, neither shall there be mourning, nor crying, nor pain anymore, for the former things have passed away." – Revelation 21:4

Chapter 47

Transition

"Beware of practicing your righteousness before other people in order to be seen by them, for then you will have no reward from your Father who is in heaven. [2]"Thus, when you give to the needy, sound no trumpet before you, as the hypocrites do in the synagogues and in the streets, that they may be praised by others. Truly, I say to you, they have received their reward. [3]But when you give to the needy, do not let your left hand know what your right hand is doing, so [4]that your giving may be in secret. And your Father who sees in secret will reward you. – Matthew 6:1-4

We all live in our own space, our own community, in what we know. When we first came to Honduras and looked at ALL the things that pulled at our heart strings and spoke to the sinful nature of man—starving families, prostituted children, lean-to houses—the needs seemed insurmountable. And in fact, they are.

I write about funny situations, frustrating situations, or ones that touch my heart. But most of the time it seems inadequate. The needs of the world are huge, but the world's needs are not mine to care for. God called our family to a little part of Honduras, and then on to the even greater needs of Equatorial Guinea, Africa, and in each place we barely scrape the surface of the overwhelming needs. But Christ did not touch every person He encountered. He did not cure the ailments of every sick person in his midst. What He did was save the world through His payment on the cross.

This is what I keep in mind when I try my hand at caring just a tiny bit for one of His. If you go into what you are doing looking for accolades or looking for the approval of man, you are going about it in all the wrong way.

So why do we write blog posts about stuff we do? Why this book? My editor asked me this question. It's a great question, and one I've actually thought a lot about. My husband is a writer—he has more than fifty published articles. He likes to share information or teach a lesson. I enjoy his articles for that reason, but it is not my preferred style to sit down and read. So when he encouraged me to write, it was his style of writing that I had in mind, and I was never inspired as I know that is not my strength. However, after writing my blog for a long time, I found a style that I enjoyed, and it taught and shared information in a very different, yet equally good way.

In addition, when Mike and I would go to churches to share what God is doing with mission work, Mike was the fact guy. He would share stats about Honduras, how many churches we built, etc.—all good things—and I would tell stories. People would come up to us after our presentation and want to know more details or more stories about what was happening. Mike finally told me that I needed to keep telling stories, because that was what caught people and what they remembered.

Time and time again I would have people, after reading a blog entry, ask me to write a book. Finally, I said yes. I would write it. I would write it because I want people to know what God is doing. It is hard, sometimes, I think, to see God's work when you are stuck in the grind of what it is to live in the U.S. I know that having done it for so long. You live your life of work, family, soccer games, etc. and go about your life without realizing that LIFE is happening. God is working, but life gets in the way.

I want people to be inspired. To be able to see God in the little things as well as the big things. To know that even in the dark jungles of Honduras, when you are doing CPR by yourself on a man who you know will never make it, that God IS sufficient. And you cling to Him. When delivering a baby by yourself in earthquake-torn Haiti, that God is sufficient. He will provide. He's got you in the palm of His hand. There is no way I could have done any of those things without Him, and I hope that shines through in the stories.

People say, "Oh my gosh. I could NEVER had done (fill in the blank)."

And I usually look back at them and say, "Yeah, me either—without God."

So, I want people to be inspired by His provision. No, things don't always turn out the way we would want them to, but the results are not our responsibility. We are simply to be God's hands and feet, and to be obedient. I want nurses to be inspired that being "just a nurse" can mean a whole lot—the difference between life and death, in some cases. That we are equipped by God, regardless of the circumstance. Give a nurse something to think outside of the box. This was not what I had in mind when I graduated nursing school—you can be sure of that! Nor was it something I thought I could even do! But here I am doing it. I want people to see that God loves the world, is active in people's lives, and He wants His children to be His light in the world. I want the stories to be a glimpse into this kind of life.

Missions is not about glamour, not *You gave up SO MUCH!* and certainly not *Wow! You accomplished so much!* It's about obedience, it's about God doing so much through us. I think I have had some unique experiences that can show these attributes of God. Sufficiency. Love. Mercy. Grace. Wisdom. Power. Holiness. Justice. Goodness. Truth. And that through Him I have seen the fruit of the Spirit in me. Love. Joy. Peace. Patience. Kindness. Goodness. Faithfulness. Gentleness. Self-Control.

I tell these stories, write my blog, and wrote this book for many reasons. My audience is part of my team. I am encouraged by, prayed for, and financially supported by my readers. The second reason I write this is for God's glory. How one small act, one simple gesture, one small box of food can make a huge and lasting impact in His people by what we do. We are all part of this huge body, the hand, the foot, the ear, the eye; and we are called to be God's hands and feet on earth, to care for His people. That is why I blog, why I write stories, why I wrote a book. That my readers may be the hands and feet that God has called us to be.

And yet I still can't help but feel inadequate. It's just little ol' me thinking I can make a difference. But the way I finally have come to see it is this: I am not here to save the world. God already did that. I am here to help that one person, that one child, and to be obedient to Him who sent me. So that's what I do—broken, sinful, inadequate, obedient me. And truly what keeps me going day after difficult day are the words I long to hear when my race is done: "Well done, my good and faithful servant."

I wrote something about the transition and my sadness in leaving Honduras to my brother. I think I was going through a "poor me" moment. I knew I had "something to show" for my time in Honduras: I left a permanent clinic and touched many lives. But would people remember me? Honestly, it doesn't matter. But in that moment, in my flesh, I cared. I hated that I saw that in myself. I had worked hard. *Who cares?* I had saved lives. *Really?! I think God did that.* Children memorized Bible verses and the catechism because I was there to teach them. *What's your point?!* I was going back and forth between my heart and my flesh.

While I was in the midst of all this personal speculation, my brother wrote something to me that truly spoke to my heart and speaks volumes to the life we live. He quoted a Greek proverb: "A society grows great when old men plant trees whose shade they know they shall never sit in."

I don't know what lives I've touched; I don't know if anyone heard the words I spoke. I don't know if the children I cuddled and gave clothing and food to will go hungry tonight, or even remember who I am. But that's not my job, that's not the thing I cling to. I cling to the hope of that shade that I pray they will have. I've planted the tree, and now I leave it to flourish.

When I die, people will likely not remember who I was or what I've done. But the tree will be there, and I pray that the roots are deep and that many shall be able to sit under its sweet shade. I am content in that I was obedient to Him who sent me.

So, we transitioned. We left what God started and will continue in Honduras. We left what He had equipped and prepared for us to do for Him and His people in Central America. And we went off to a new adventure. A more challenging and difficult one. One that He spent time preparing us for. Off to the land that, in our new teammate's words, "chews up and spits out missionaries." Off to a land that has the feeling of permanent camping—bad water, inconsistent electricity, severe poverty, and medical and social injustice. We went because God had called us to go to this new place.

"I will instruct you and teach you in the way you should go;
I will counsel you with my eye upon you." – Psalm 32:8

Chapter 48

Africa

Bleary-eyed, I looked out the window of the airplane with a mixture of relief, horror, disbelief, and amazement as we arrived after over thirty-six hours of travel. We had landed in Malabo, the island capitol city of the tiny country of Equatorial Guinea, Africa. We were almost to our final destination. One more flight would get us to the mainland city of Bata, which is where we were headed. I hoisted up my skirt; wiped off my already sweaty brow; grabbed my carry-on bag, purse, pillow and iPad; and headed out the door. I was immediately met with the oppressive heat of the sweatbox that was to be our new home, and it was only seven thirty in the morning.

I lived in Honduras for almost eight years as a missionary nurse. I had come mentally and physically prepared for what lay ahead. Or so I thought.

Chapter 49

Feeling Alone

"Fear not, for I am with you; be not dismayed, for I am your God; I will strengthen you, I will help you, I will uphold you with my righteous right hand." – Isaiah 41:10

That moment when you feel like you are all alone: people speaking a language you don't understand, eating food you don't know, wearing clothes that don't feel natural. You don't have a car, you take showers with a hose, you cook on a stove you don't get with food you aren't sure about. You only wear dresses or skirts, eat and breathe sweat, and suffer with electricity that is questionable at best. You can't even figure out where to throw your trash, or how to get rid of the flying cockroaches and the deadly mosquitoes. The water is deadly, the snakes can kill, and invisible lurking microbes want to invade your body. There is no transportation, you are six to eight time zones away from those you love, the stores are closed for half the day, and food costs more than in the States.

That is the reality of missions. We read books and watch movies about it, and it all seems so glamorous. Even our time in Honduras seemed like it was easy. But reality struck when we reached Africa. The honeymoon was over. We were told more than once, "Equatorial Guinea chews up missionaries and spits them out." No one stays. Africa is no joke.

Galadriel: "You are a ring-bearer, Frodo. To bear a ring of power is to be alone. This task was appointed to you. And if you do not find a way, no one will."—*The Fellowship of the Ring*

When Frodo says he cannot accomplish his task on his own, Galadriel responds with the quotation above. She means to encourage him, but also to let him know that his journey has just begun. The fellowship has given him a start, but the task ahead is his and his alone. He no longer needs the others, and, indeed, he separates from them at the end. These words also serve as a warning for Frodo, alerting him to the solitude he'll struggle with as long as he has the ring. Frodo will wrestle with solitude even after he's destroyed the ring and returned to the Shire.

We left Honduras. We started there from scratch, created a team, ministry, and a family. Then we left it, and we left those behind and haven't heard from them since. They have moved on. I guess we have too.

I left my family behind as well. Both of my parents have passed away, my daughter is in college pursuing her dream, and my in-laws are in Sacramento. My best friends are continents and huge time zones away.

My husband and I travel this path alone.

And at times it feels so very alone. Let's face it, we cling to what we know. We cling to our church friends, our best friends, even our favorite coffee shops. But remove ALL that you know, and when you are left with nothing familiar, not even the language or food or the comfort of reliable electricity and a hot shower that you can step into, you are left with what you cling to. And so, I cling to my Savior. He is sufficient for me in my spirit.

But in my flesh I am human, and so I long for things I don't have. I am weak, and in that, He is strong. I know that this is a season, and that He will meet me in my deepest needs. I cry out to Him, and He responds in kind.

"And after you have suffered a little while, the God of all grace, who has called you to his eternal glory in Christ, will himself restore, confirm, strengthen, and establish you." - 1 Peter 5:10

Chapter 50

Termites Ate My Couch

"All winged insects that go on all fours are detestable to you." – Leviticus 11:20

We arrived at our new home in Africa, in this little country called Equatorial Guinea, which is the only Spanish-speaking country in Africa. It was pretty cool, I might add, that we were able to be understood the first day we arrived. But, as Africa would soon teach us, we had lessons to learn. Within an hour of our arrival, we lost electricity. We had arrived somewhat prepared, with battery-powered headlamps, flashlights, and a lantern. We wanted to check in with friends and family and let everyone know we had arrived safely. So our teammates let us borrow their USB key which gave us internet capabilities. Basically, you use cell towers to get your internet, and it is SLOW.

I was also just starting two new classes for my master's degree. I was on a school calendar that was not all that forgiving, and, believe it or not, I had two assignments I had to turn in. I had been working on them while we were in transit, so they were done by the time we arrived in country, but they had to be uploaded onto the university's site to be counted. So, once Mike had posted our status on Facebook and sent private messages to everyone who needed to know we had arrived, he handed me the key so I could upload my assignments. We were sitting on the floor, in the dark with just the glow of our computer screens and our tiny little flashlight. I was trying to log on, when I suddenly felt something move by my leg. Not wanting to let my imagination get the best of me, I just swatted at whatever "imaginary" thing had run by my leg, and continued uploading my assignments, until the two-inch cockroach decided that the opening in my shorts was the perfect place to hang out. This nightmare scrambled into my shorts. To my complete dismay, I jumped up and screamed like a little girl, frantically swatting at my shorts while at the same time trying to completely disrobe. I knew what it was, I knew it to my core, but I didn't want to know what I knew. There was a freaking cockroach in my pants.

The stupid bug managed to get out and I went on the hunt. *Oh no you don't!* No WAY will that thing be in here when I'm trying to sleep. So with headlamp on and shoe in hand, I hunted and destroyed the thing that had greeted me on my first night in Africa.

Heart rate and respiratory rate returning back to normal, we proceeded to settle ourselves down to our first night in Africa. With mosquito nets hung and our tiny little bed made, we looked at each other, still trying to grasp the fact that we had finally arrived.

Gratefully we made it alive through the night. Even with the electricity coming and going, which meant fans starting and stopping, we did manage to grab a decent amount of sleep. Thirty-six hours of travel will make that happen.

The next morning, we got up to take stock of what was in our little 800-square-foot house. The property manager had told us that whatever was in the house was ours to use. We were actually really happy about this because it meant that our first week wasn't going to be quite as frantic as we thought. We still had a refrigerator, stove, desk, bed, all kitchen stuff, etc. to buy, but we could get by in the first week with the small bed, single table, and couch that had been left for us.

We wanted to devise a plan for the household goods we needed to purchase. There is no use of credit cards here—everything is 100% cash only. But we couldn't believe the prices of things! The sticker shock was incredible! Basically, everything was considerably more expensive than the same item in the States. We actually got a monthly stipend raise in moving from Honduras to Africa. Equatorial Guinea is considerably poorer than Honduras, but way more expensive. It doesn't make sense, but there you have it.

We had money to use for start-up expenses, but we realized we weren't going to have enough after all. So we started itemizing everything that was in the house, and basically determined that what was in the house was going to have to stay. We couldn't afford to replace what was there. We simply didn't have the funds. So the really ugly couch was going to have to stay.

All right, I thought, *I'll figure out a way to cover it, or get new cushions, or something, because as it is, we will never use it.* Within a few days, I was tired of sitting on the hard, plastic chairs around our plastic table, so I thought I would settle myself on to the couch and just take a moment to think. So, I sat down—and the entire side of the couch collapsed. What the WHAT?! I quickly got up, and looked down—there was termite dust all around the bottom portion of the couch. After having lived in Honduras for almost eight years, I was very accustomed to what termite dust looked like. They are everywhere—any place in your house that has wood, they are going to be in. It's just part of life there. Well clearly, it was going to be part of life here as well.

So, I looked at Mike, and the thought was very clear on my face: *I want to trash or burn this couch NOW!* But if we got rid of it, we couldn't replace it. So I found some spare wood and propped up the side of the couch, and there it sits to this day, pretty much not sat upon, just taking up space. And the termites are having a field day I'm sure!

"Then God said, "Let Us make man in Our image, according to Our likeness; and let them rule over the fish of the sea and over the birds of the sky and over the cattle and over all the earth, and over every creeping thing that creeps on the earth." – Genesis 1:26

Chapter 51

Water crisis

"But whoever drinks of the water that I will give him will never be thirsty again. The water that I will give him will become in him a spring of water welling up to eternal life." – John 4:14

Africa, Week 3: Arrival seemed somewhat uneventful as we slowly accustomed ourselves to the unbearable heat, equatorial living, power outages, water shortages, and downpours. Today was an exciting day! My washing machine was going to be delivered! I had been relying upon the good graces of my teammate and the hard work of their housekeeper to wash our clothes. At forty-eight, I really wanted to be independent and not rely on someone else to wash my underwear!

The guys bringing the washing machine lifted it with one hand each and dropped it off in our patio area. As I took the cardboard off of the brand new machine, I studied it. *Hmmm...what does "semi-automatic" washing machine mean?* I read the meager instructions, and my eyes got bigger and bigger. Ah, I get it now...

As I was getting water from the spicket at the side of the house and filling up a bucket, my sweet neighbor motioned for me to stop. My neighbors were missionaries as well. He was from Costa Rica, and his new wife was from Chile. Both were Spanish speakers and super sweet. As we really did not receive any type of orientation upon our arrival, we didn't realize the serious water crisis that the property had. There was one well that served three families.

As my neighbor approached me, she said, "We hate to tell you, but this water can't be used to wash clothes. You need to go get water from the well at the end of the property to use for wash."

I knew there was another well. I also knew it was at the end of the property right near the swamp that (at least in my mind's eye) was full of anacondas, certainly tons of mosquitos (true) and any number of critters that wanted to eat me at any minute. *You have got to be kidding me!* I thought.

So my day that started out as one of joy quickly became one of realizing another new reality of what my life was going to look like. I grabbed Mike, and we headed down to the well at the end of the hill. We opened up the top, lowered the bucket down, and hauled up two buckets of water to fill the big bucket we had brought. It took both of us to carry it back up the hill; he grabbed one side and I grabbed the other.

Up the hill we walked, dumped the water into the washing machine, and headed back down the hill. The second bucketful we once again dumped into the washing machine, and then we went back down the hill. Two more times we made this trip, but the next two buckets we put into a large fifty-gallon ethyl alcohol drum that we had purchased just the day before for water storage. This water I would use for my rinse cycle.

Now I was ready. I grabbed my sheets and towels and put them into the washing machine. I turned the dial to "wash/rinse," added detergent to the water already in the tub, and set the timer on the machine to "15." And the washer started. It basically was an agitator. It turned clockwise, then counterclockwise. Promptly fifteen minutes later, my timer went off, and the machine stopped. I grabbed the drainage tube and pointed it down the hill, turned the dial to "drain," and waited while the tub drained. The tub was now empty except for my clean laundry. Dipping the bucket into the blue drum, I pulled up enough water to fill my tub, turned the dial back to "wash/rinse," set the timer to fifteen and sat down. More agitating.

The timer went off, I opened the lid, set the dial to "drain," and waited for all the water to run out again. Now what? There was a second chamber on my washing machine. I opened it up, and it was the spinner to spin off the excess water. However, I had already been warned never to overload it as it would break the part on the bottom of the chamber. So I started to wring out the clothes by hand as I transferred them to the spin chamber. However, only about half my load would fit. So I set the spin dial to five minutes and sat down. Once the spin cycle was done, I removed the clothes into my waiting basket, and wrung out the second half of clothes, putting them into the spinner. I sat down to wait for the five-minute spin. When the spinning finished, I put the clothes into my basket, and headed up the hill to the clotheslines that are on the property and available for anyone to use.

I threw my king-size top sheet on the farthest line, only to stop. I looked at the filth that was just transferred to my sheet, and honestly, almost started crying. SERIOUSLY?! The clotheslines were metal; it should have occurred to me that there was a chance there could be rust on them, but it hadn't. So I grabbed my pillowcase and sacrificed it to the cause. I ran the pillowcase over the two lines I was going to use, removing the majority of the dirt and rust that had accumulated over time.

I hung my laundry and looked at my pillowcase. *Now what?*

Down by the well there was a conveniently located hand-wash station, complete with a built-in washboard. Mike had mistakenly purchased what he thought was a solid piece of dish soap, which in reality was soap for hand washing. So, I grabbed that and headed back down the hill. I went to the well and got a full bucket of water. Then I took my bar of soap and bucket of water, and commenced to scrub my pillowcase on the washboard until it was clean. Another bucket of water later, my pillowcase was fully rinsed and ready to be hung. I trekked back up the hill and put my freshly washed pillowcase on the line.

About an hour later I went up the hill to check on my laundry. It was dry, but there was still another step that needed to be done. Equatorial Guinea has these nasty bot flies that lay their larvae into damp clothes. When you put these clothes on, the larvae hatch and burrow into your skin. And it grows and matures in your skin before it burrows back out as a fly, and continues on its lifecycle. It is quite disgusting and painful. No thank you! So the last ten minutes of the laundry process is to put the clothes in the dryer to heat the larvae and kill them. With clothes dry, bug-free, and folded, I moved on to the next task at hand.

About an hour later, Mike called me into the kitchen. The voltage regulator wasn't working. Electricity here fluctuates so much that it eventually destroys whatever is plugged into it. Because of this, anything we have that is valuable we plug into a voltage regulator. Well, my dryer had fried the voltage regulator. So now the refrigerator hadn't been running, nor had anything else that was plugged into the regulator. We swapped out the regulator for another one and got everything plugged back in. But I looked at Mike and shook my head. What were we going to do? We couldn't burn out a regulator every time we did laundry and we couldn't burn out our dryer. We had to come up with a better plan. Ultimately, we had to hire an electrician who installed a separate breaker and a separate electric line just for the dryer.

"Then he showed me a river of the water of life, clear as crystal, coming from the throne of God and of the Lamb, in the middle of its street. [2]On either side of the river was the tree of life, bearing twelve kinds of fruit, yielding its fruit every month; and the leaves of the tree were for the healing of the nations." – Revelation 22:1-2

Chapter 52

Exorcism

Service at the little church we attend started like any other. We looked forward to a time of praise and worship, announcements, and preaching. But that's where things went off kilter unexpectedly and pretty fast. There were a few women at the front of church asking for prayer, one holding her six-month-old child in her arms. Before prayer could even start, the woman started screaming and convulsing. Another woman swept in to grab her child before she was flung across the room. The woman raised her arms as if she were a marionette being held up by the strings, and she started to be flung around the room. She continued screaming, in a tongue I didn't recognize. Her convulsions brought her to her knees, and she hit the floor screaming in the unknown tongue. The pastor of the church ran to her, swinging his crutches as fast as he could. The pastor's body is afflicted with cerebral palsy, but he never lets his physical disability slow him down. Flinging his crutches aside, he grasped the woman's head and spoke to her. He asked in Spanish, "What is your name?"

"Soy Satanas!" ("I am Satan!") she responded in a voice from the grave. Then she lifted up her head and in a voice that brought chills up my spine she said, "Where is my bride? Why don't you follow my disciples?"

The pastor replied, "NO! You are a bride of Christ. LEAVE HER! In the name of Christ, I command you to LEAVE her!"

The young woman looked at him with crazed eyes and a crooked smile and repeated, "Soy Satanas!"

I know what this sounds like. I get it. I'm a white-bread, upper-middle class California girl from the good ol' U.S. of A. This kind of stuff just doesn't happen. And yet it does.

This was not my first encounter with elements of that nature. I first encountered it on a trip to the Philippines. I entered a room and was surrounded by an evil presence so heavy that I tore open my Bible and started singing the Psalms out loud. While I was in Honduras, I was physically attacked by a woman who pounded my head against the ground and tried to gouge out my eyes because she said she could see demons. I saw a young woman fling five adult men across the room and speak in a language she had never spoken before. Ask any missionary who has been around and you will hear story after story— things you just simply can't make up.

So, trust me when I say this, I am a believer. Just because you don't hear about it doesn't make it not so. I am here to bring to light things of that world. So I sat there, in my pew, with tears streaming down my face as I felt the burden of the darkness in this place. I felt how present Satan was here in this country. I have seen the witch doctors as they ply their wares, seen the totems they place, and the dances they dance. And yet, I saw the church rally around this young woman. I saw the pastor reaching out to her spiritually and physically. I sat and prayed and cried for this country, and for so many other countries that live in darkness without the Savior. I did not feel fear. For I also wholeheartedly believe that if you are indwelt by the Holy Spirit, you cannot be indwelt by a demon. Sure, believers can be pestered and bothered by them, but because of the Seal on their souls, they are freed of that.

The pastor asked my husband to come to the front and pray with him. He grabbed her head again and said, "In the name of Christ, I COMMAND you to leave her!"

She growled and talked in a nonsensical voice.

"In the name of Christ, I COMMAND you to leave her!" He turned to the congregation and said, "She is filled with demons. We must pray for her!" The congregation started to pray, to sing, to lift up this woman to Him who could do all. Then the pastor turned his attention back to her.

This process continued, the woman screaming and yelling out profanities, while the pastor rebuked the demons, holding the face of the woman and telling her to come back, to be the bride of Christ. All in all, about thirty minutes went by while the woman was wracked by continued convulsions, and the pastor continued to banish the demons. Then she collapsed. It was as if her marionette body had its strings clipped, and she was released. The pastor leapt to his feet proclaiming the victory in Christ, and the congregation rejoiced with him and broke out in song.

The tears dried on my face, and I took a deep breath. The headache that had been threatening to come hit full force. I grabbed my Bible and was ready to leave. As we said our farewells and slowly walked back home, my heart continued to be heavy. Mike and I talked with a friend who had joined us that day. It was her first experience with something like this, and we shared with her our other experiences. When I got home, I took some Tylenol, made sandwiches for lunch, and started to write. I needed to put it to paper to help me process the experience.

Chapter 53

The Eagles and the Pineapples

Leaving the house at 9 a.m., we thought we would have sufficient time to get where we were going. We arranged transportation by a local taxi driver who knew how to get there, negotiated a price, and away we went.

Travel through the "big" town of Bata can be a little cumbersome as there are police check points all throughout town where you can be randomly stopped to check that "all your papers are in order." But we hadn't experienced travel outside of Bata yet. We were in for a few surprises. Within the first ten miles we had already passed through four military or police checkpoints. We were required to show our passports at each station, were asked questions at every stop, and even had to get out and present ourselves at a few.

We were five hours into our supposedly four-hour drive, and we had just arrived at the future capital of the country, Mongomo. The current president is originally from this very small pueblo. He wants to move the capitol from the island city to the mainland and relocate it in his home village. It seems so oddly out of place, far into the interior of the country, and clearly without enough population or wealth to make this strange city work. It's not officially open for business, but you can see future government buildings, a presidential palace, and a 500-person hotel (with no guests).

It was then that our taxi driver notified us of a few things. First, he didn't get the travel papers he was supposed to have to drive out here, so he was going to rely on his "negotiation money" (his word, not "bribe,") to get him through the checkpoints. Apparently, it had worked, at least so far.

The second thing he confessed to us was that he really had no idea how to get where we were going. We told him to figure it out. We had only been in country for two and a half months, and we certainly didn't know the area. After talking to four different people on the street, we thought we knew where we were going.

An hour later, and now six hours into our "four-hour drive," we arrived into Nsork, or Nsok, or N'sork, or Nzork—all ways we saw it spelled, which didn't make finding it on a map very easy. We pulled up to the pastor's house where we were going to be staying, and then our driver dropped another surprise on us. "If I go back to Bata," he said, "I'm not coming back. This is much farther than I thought, it's risky, and I can't drive at night."

To say we were shocked and quite perturbed would be an understatement. We were totally at his mercy, and he knew it. So, for the next thirty minutes, my husband and he negotiated what was going to happen. We ended up having to pay for his hotel stay and an additional full day's wage in order for him to stay to take us back four days later.

As we were on the way into the house, a large truck passed by on the street and managed to catch the electric wire that ran to the house. The truck didn't stop, pulled down the cord, and the electricity went out. It was dusk at this point, but being well-prepared missionaries, we had brought our flashlights and headlamps with us just in case. The family pulled out their oil lamps, and we were good to go.

The bed in our room was a three-inch foam mattress with a sheet on top. There was no blanket; it was simply too hot. We had a mosquito net to put around us, and a window that didn't have a screen. With no fan in the room and no screen on the window, we knew we were going to be in for some hot nights.

The family we were staying with was a pastor, his wife, and their seven children. The wife was pregnant with their eighth, and their eldest daughter was pregnant with her first. The eldest daughter was scheduled to have her baby before her mom. The culture here is to have a lot of children. An average household of ten children is typical.

At dinner the culture learning began. The pastor called us in to dinner, and my husband, my daughter, and I sat down with the pastor at the table. No one else joined us. Not his wife, nor any of his children. We enjoyed the very tipico Guinean meal, had some small conversation, then went to bed. As we were lying in bed, we discussed what we experienced over dinner. It was very clear that we had a definite learning curve we had to figure out fast. By the end of the week, we got it, but it wasn't without a few serious cultural faux pas.

The first faux pas was to offer the pastor money for our stay. Our team leader had told us to bring money to give to the pastor, but unfortunately, it wasn't explained exactly how to make that happen. When we offered the money to him, he said, "We are Fang. We take care of our guests." And he refused the money. Whoops, we knew we hadn't done that right. But we knew we still needed to give him some money for our stay, so we just needed to figure out how to make it culturally appropriate to do that. My husband ultimately found a way that didn't show offense, and the pastor was honored to receive the money. Mike said that he wanted to contribute toward his salary. Money exchanged hands. So it wasn't the actual accepting of money that was the problem, it was the perception of why it was being given that was important.

The other thing we learned is that to be a guest in a Fang household is to be in a place of honor. Because of that position, the children and the wife eat apart. The guests are to be honored. We also ended up having a number of meals alone as the pastor headed to work or didn't join us for a meal, and no one else did. But that was okay, and we understood. Another thing I had a hard time with was I was not allowed to clean the table or help with the dishes. This was to honor the guests, so I had to let that go as well.

The next thing to maneuver was the water situation. Potable water, and even just access to water, is a huge problem in the country. This pueblo had no running water, no wells, and no access to potable water at all. Thankfully, the pastor had a car and was able to drive the thirty minutes to the neighboring community to use their water station to collect potable water for his family. Because of the difficulty of getting water, all bathing and washing of clothes and dishes were done in the closest river. The entire community used this small river. There are many things I will do in the name of being a good missionary. However, when things threaten my health or my life, I am very careful about it. There is a serious problem here with River Blindness or Onchocerciasis. This disease is caused from the bite of a fly that is very common along the river banks. The fly deposits thousands of larvae into the human body where it can affect the skin and the eyes. This condition can eventually lead to blindness. According to the World Health Organization, about fifty percent of men over forty in West African communities are blinded by this disease. I forbade Madison or Mike to go down to the river to bathe. I've eaten all sorts of questionable foods and have consumed many a drink made with "potable" water that was not so potable, but this I wasn't willing to risk. Call me a bad missionary, or call it making a judgment call. I was totally okay with going without a shower or bath for four days in the name of keeping us healthy.

The bathroom was another interesting factor. I find bathrooms throughout the world to be very indicative of the culture. I've used bathrooms that are just a hole in the floor, with marked outlines around the hole so you know where to place your feet. I've been in one of the most expensive airports in the world and found a drain hole on the bottom of each stall, with no toilet paper to be found and a hose with a sprayer attached to the end. I've been in locations where there are no toilets, and you sit next to a wall or find the closest large rock to go behind. I've been in outside latrines with a few sticks as privacy screens. So bathrooms don't stress me out, instead I find them quite interesting. This bathroom was quite nice, but tiny. The sink, the toilet, and a tiny tiled area that served as a shower were the only things inside the bathroom. I use the term shower, but with no running water, I assumed it was just used for bucket showers if water was available. When I first sat down on the toilet, I quickly discovered that I was much too tall to actually sit on the toilet. My legs hit the wall right in front of me, so I had to sit sideways on the toilet. This was a house with no running water, and the bucket of precious water next to the toilet was for flushing. I tried to conserve as much water as possible, since the pastor had to go to the next town to replenish their water supply.

When we slid into bed under the mosquito net, we felt the full reality of what sleeping here for the next four nights was going to be like. The three-inch foam provided almost no cushion, the pillows were totally flat, and the mosquito netting provided almost no protection against the many nasty critters that were determined to get through. Mosquito netting without permethrin is almost worthless. Permethrin is this amazing, natural ingredient that kills mosquitos. You might think the netting would be enough to keep them from you, but what happens when you roll over in the middle of the night and your arm is right next to the mosquito netting? The smart little mosquito just bites you through the netting. If, however, your net is dipped in permethrin, when the mosquito lands to bite you and inject its awful critters into your body, it dies instead. But here we were, lying under the netting, with mosquitoes hovering all around us.

So with the sound of mosquitos circling and sweat pouring down our bodies, we attempted to go to sleep. Within about thirty minutes, I could hear the deep breathing of my husband as his exhausted body said enough was enough. With my headphones on, listening to the quiet sounds of country music, I started to drift off to sleep until this blood-curdling scream awoke me. If you have ever been startled out of sleep you will understand the complete disorientation and confusion that confronts you. I sat bolt up in bed and said, "What?! What's wrong?"

My husband was MAD! A lizard had landed on his head and crawled across his face. In self-preservation he batted at this monstrosity and flung it across the bed. You may be thinking about the nice little lizards that eat bugs in your backyard, that your kids try and catch, that you may have put on your ear lobes as mock earrings. These are not those kind of lizards. Equatorial Guinea is teeming with six- to twelve-inch lizards. They thrive in this bug-ridden country. They are everywhere! We have them in our ceiling, and there are probably more than twenty I can see at any given time of the day around our property—and that's just the ones I can see. Somehow this six-inch lizard had made its way under our mosquito netting, climbed up, and plopped down on my husband's face. Because I was the ever-ready missionary, with my flashlight next to my head, I flicked it on and chased down the lizard, opened our door, and shooed it out.

It took a good hour for us to settle back down and attempt to fall asleep—sweating, with the buzzing of the mosquitos circling our net, waiting for their next meal.

Morning came, and the three of us were invited to eat at the table by ourselves. (The pastor had already left for his job.) We consumed our delicious meal and were ready for the day. Mike waited at the house, hoping the pastor would return, which he did, so Mike went with him to go lay cement.

Madison and I decided we would walk around the community. I spied some kids walking down a street that was being cleared for new pavement. They looked like they were on a mission, so we followed them. We were quite the spectacle, Madison and I, being "blancas" (white people), so the kids had to stop and stare. But when I started speaking Spanish to them, they knew that I was somehow okay.

We stayed behind them to see where they were going and came upon the river where everyone goes. It is the only source of water, for bathing, for washing clothes, for cleaning dishes. It was a river I would not go near, but it was all they had.

The kids pulled off their clothes, washed them, washed themselves, and even took the time to play for a little bit. Not wanting to disturb their time, we kept going. Madison and I walked about three miles in different directions, observing the community, seeing women at work, watching children playing and people living their lives. Just taking the time to make observations is such an important work as a missionary. It allows you time to reflect and understand the culture.

Mike sent me a text on my phone: food was being prepared for us to eat. So, Madison and I returned to the house. When we arrived, the pastor's children were playing in the front of the house. Soon more children arrived to play. The beauty of not having television, computers, PlayStations, Wiis, or any other type of electronic device to occupy your time is that playing is all about playing. It's been a long time since I was a kid, but I do have a few tricks up my sleeve. For one thing, I can do origami. Kids love seeing the magic of a piece of paper coming to life and becoming something else. Two things I excel at are the flapping bird and cootie catcher. So, I made both, and many of them. I showed the kids how to make them, and without my assistance, they were able to make more. We played the hand-slap game, my daughter got a game of sharks and minnows going, followed by duck-duck-goose, and rock/paper/scissors. These were all totally new games to them, and they loved them!

For the next three hours we watched the kids in amazement. They had more games under their belt then I had in my entire childhood, and I grew up during a time without handheld gaming devices. The only time there was a pause in the activity was when they were deciding which game to play next.

One of these games we watched and tried, without success, to figure out. Finally, when the sun was going down and kids were being called to go home, we asked the significance of the game.

Two people were farmers. Two people were eagles. The rest were pineapples. The kids who were pineapples gathered in a circle and called out to the farmers to come see if they were ready to be picked. The farmers would go from child to child and push on their back to see if they were sturdy, smack them with branches to see if they were strong, and if they were, they would sample the pineapple and decide that they were, indeed, ready to be picked. They would then leave the area, and two eagles would arrive upon the scene and steal the pineapples that the farmers had decided were ready to be picked. When the farmers returned, they would ask the other pineapples what had happened to their ripened pineapples. When they found that they had been taken by the eagles, they went in a circle again to find the next pineapples that were ready for consumption. And so, the game went until all the pineapples were gone. Finally the farmers, in frustration, would seek out the house of the eagles to take their pineapples back. But the pineapples were happy to be free from the farmers and the eagles, so they would scatter and hide. It was then that the farmers would try and find the pineapples and other items to gather to take back to their farms.

This was such an interesting game. It really was more of a story told in game format. I tried to do a little research to find out if this was a folk legend or a fable, but no one seemed to know the origin of the story.

The kids played, danced, sang, and entertained themselves until it was too dark to go on. I looked around at the gathered children, and did not see a single child that was overweight. And it's no wonder—the amount of calories burned in simply playing was incredible. I did see the underlying malnutrition, the lighter hair, the pot-belly children from lack of protein, but I saw children living and enjoying life. A team that came down to Honduras one year was really struggling with the level of poverty. I even had one lady ask me, "Do they know how poor they are?"

It was a good question, and one that I think all of us need to evaluate. I do not think they know how poor they are. This is their life. This is how they live, how their parents lived, and how their grandparents lived. They are often hungry, bathe in a contaminated river, drive thirty miles for potable water, and lack basic healthcare. But in that, they are happy, they have a family that loves them, siblings to play with, and a God who cares for them.

It was a humbling experience. I had pinched a nerve in my neck right before we left, so I was burdened with headaches, horrible sleeping, stiffness in my neck, and dehydration. I was filthy, but through it all I saw the beauty that surrounded me. A family that cared for each other, people who loved God, a community that blessed those around them. It was a beautiful thing!

That night we went to visit Maria, the pastor's mother-in-law. She was a seventy-year-old woman and the matriarch of a family of ten, with, as she put it, "I'm not sure...20 or 30 grandchildren, and some great-grandchildren as well."

The pastor took us to her humble home, not ten minutes from the pueblo we were staying in. There is no electricity to this community, and no running water. Her small shack was four walls with a dirt floor, and openings, but no doors. She cooks over a fire she has in her house. These were some of the most amazing and basic living standards I'd ever seen. Her bed was sticks of wood over a frame, and a small foam cushion. She had all ten of her children in this little home, and only speaks Fang. She is a woman who looks ninety, but is seventy. She lives a hard life. Daily she goes to collect wood for her stove and hand wash her clothes in the river. She has never known a life of running water and electricity. She has never had a drink with ice in it or known the hands of a physician when she delivers a child into the world. She has never slept one night unmolested by mosquitos, lizards, moths, and other critters that invade her sleep. But she has loved mightily, lived beautifully, and passed on her strength of character to her children. We ended the night sharing a pineapple from the garden behind her house. After giving her the proper head-bumping good-bye, we went on our way.

Please Lord Jesus, help me remember that my first world problems are only that, and that even some of my third world problems are not anything like what my sweet friend Maria lives with on a daily basis.

At the end of our time, our taxi driver showed back up to the house, and we began the trek back to our home in Bata. At the last military checkpoint (the fourteenth—I counted), we had turned over our passports to the officer and were waiting for them to be returned, when this guy carrying a huge dead rat caught the eye of our taxi driver. He gestured the man over, and they began to talk in Fang. I could tell there was finagling of price, and finally it was settled. Holding the rat by the tail, the vender handed it over to our taxi driver, who put it in the trunk of the car. When he returned, I had to ask.

"It's medicine," he said, "African medicine."

My curiosity deepened. I asked what kinds of illnesses it fixed. "We take the bones and cook them or boil them, then put them in our children's milk to make them strong. It's better," he continued, "if you can help them before they are born. If you take monkey bones and feed them to the mother, or boil them and consume them as a soup, then the bones make the growing baby strong. Then, by the time they are five you will see it—they can climb like a monkey they are so strong!"

This is the kind of thing I wanted to know about. This was a young man in his late twenties who grew up in the big city, but African "medicine" was ingrained in his daily life.

We got our passports back and continued on the last few miles to our home. My husband looked at me and said, "I can't wait to get back to the 'comforts' of our home!"

And then we both laughed hysterically! We live in a home where we collect rainwater to drink, flush our toilets with a bucket, take camp showers, and wonder about electricity—and we were excited about this! The little things that we call our creature comforts are truly a matter of perspective. It reminds me that others have it even more difficult than I do. So when I start to complain about hanging my clothes under a mosquito netting, I remind myself to be grateful that I at least have a permethrin-treated mosquito netting to put them under.

Chapter 54

Things You Miss
and
Things You Take for Granted

There are certain conveniences that we are accustomed to. If you were suddenly thrown into a new circumstance, it would be hard. Think of your life as you live it now. You live in a climate-controlled house, wake up to your coffee already brewed in your automatic coffeepot, take a hot shower, and get ready for work. You walk out to your garage, hit the automatic door opener, climb into your climate-controlled car, and use your back-up camera to steer out of your garage. On the drive to work you stop by the drive-through coffee place, sliding your debit card in the machine, and get another coffee for the road. You listen to the news on the way to work, check your e-mail with your voice-activated Bluetooth phone attachment system. You know you won't have a chance to pick up those groceries on your way home, so you jump online and order your groceries to be delivered when you arrive home. You pop your prepared food into the oven, and thirty minutes later you sit down to a yummy meal with your family and talk about your day. You've already put your laundry in the washer, so when the timer goes off, so you switch it to the dryer and sit back down. You pop open a bottle of wine and sit with your spouse on the couch to watch the evening news, while checking your e-mail on your wicked-fast internet. Then you set your house alarm and head off to your bed that is not surrounded by mosquito netting and settle down for the night. This, my friends, described my daily routine when I lived in the States. And I know I'm describing a similar situation for most of us.

That's what it is to live in the U.S. We love our culture, and that is 100% totally okay—until, after forty years, you are removed from that situation and placed in a brand-new environment like we experience here in Africa. Let me share some of what that is like:

Running water: We are on a well system with a pump/tank setup. Low water table = no water to pump to tank = no water in the house.

Flush toilet: Because of our water rationing (we are limited to thirty liters of water per day), we don't fill the tank with water. Instead we have a bucket next to the toilet so we can limit the amount of water. We live by the motto: "If it's yellow, let it mellow; if it's brown, flush it down."

Dishwasher: That's me. I haven't had a dishwasher for nine years, and I won't lie—I miss it.

Hot water: Well water / rain water = no hot water.

Warm shower (heck, a shower): We have a hand-held faucet hooked up to the well water, which we typically can't use because we would have to switch it on or off due to our water restrictions. Instead we have a camp shower that we fill with 1 ¼ gallons of water to take a shower. That's it—that's all we get.

A car: The impracticality of a car (bribes, cost) means no car and 100% reliance upon public transportation. So think about your most recent trip to the grocery store and imagine you had to put all your groceries in a bag to throw over your shoulder, hike out to get a taxi, and then carry them down the hill to your house. It means you go shopping a LOT.

Potable water: All our water must be filtered. There is no company around that provides potable water, so you either purchase one liter bottles at the store; go down to one of the four filling stations around town that supposedly provides chlorinated, but not filtered, water; or you filter and sanitize your own water. That's what we do. Every faucet has a filter on it, and our drinking water goes through a double-filter process.

TV: I'm not going to lie. I like vegging out in front of the TV after a long, stressful day. I love to watch the news, and there have always been a few shows we love. There are only two TV stations in country, both run by the government, so honestly, we aren't interested.

Internet: Oh the joy of fast internet. We only have 3G, using a cell card for our internet. And to call it 3G is being way too generous. It is impossible to stream anything, and to download something like a show off of iTunes takes anywhere from one to three days.

Fruit: Our choices here are papaya, mango, and pineapple. You can get oranges, but they are imported, so they cost more than two dollars apiece. It is the same with apples; they are available, but almost cost prohibitive. And the one time I bought a watermelon, I spent twelve dollars because I really wanted it. I miss cherries, strawberries, nectarines, peaches, blueberries, blackberries, and pomegranates. I miss pears, Gala apples, Fuji apples, and Cuties. I think you get the idea.

Clothing: Finding clothing that fits me as a 6'1" tall woman in the U.S. can be challenging, but here, it's not even an option. So all the clothes I wear are things I brought with me, and if I need more, I have to wait for a trip back to the States.

Convenience: They have a true siesta here. The grocery stores are closed from one o'clock to four o'clock, Monday through Friday; only open half a day on Saturday; and closed on Sunday. It means you have to plan very carefully. Nothing is premade or partially prepared; everything has to be made with original ingredients, from scratch.

Education: We knew going on the mission field was going to have a huge impact on the education of our daughter. As much as we complain in the U.S., we have great public education. We knew that we were going to have to be okay with the best that Honduras had to offer. There was a choice of homeschooling, but we wanted our daughter to be a part of the Honduran culture, learn the language, and have Honduran friends. We felt that by homeschooling her we would be setting her apart from that. For our family, that was the best decision we could make, even knowing that her schooling was going to be less than she would have received in the States.

Red Meat: The food of choice here is chicken. It's on the course for every meal, that or fish. But red meat? Nope. Not unless you want to purchase the Cebu that is at the butcher shop. But after the few times we saw birds pecking at the meat, we decided that this was not going to be an option. If anyone knows me well, they know I'm a lover of steak! I don't have it often, but I do enjoy a nine-ounce, medium-rare filet mignon. Yum! And forget the "fresh" bush meat at the market. No way!

Radio: Once in a while, when the internet is being nice, I am able to play iHeartRadio and listen to my country music. But that's only on good days. Otherwise, I'm stuck with the handful of songs I have on my computer. Time to make a trip to the States and download new music!

Movies: Mike and I are movie fanatics! We always see new releases and make a date night at least once a month to see a movie. We are always up-to-date on the latest and greatest. My friends knew to ask me about a movie, because they assumed I had seen it. Here—well, there isn't a movie theater in the entire country. Nothing...nada. Our trips to the States are going to be full of movie-watching date nights.

Health: I won't say we get sick that often, but when we do, our healthcare is up to us. I've been able to take care of most things. I'm the family doctor for our little family. The local public hospital is off limits to us. I've been there as a visitor, and there is no way I'll go there as a patient. We would never use it. The two private hospitals have seen better days. If we get into trouble with a serious illness, we will have to head back to the States for treatment.

Washing machine: If you read the chapter about my washing machine, you know what I'm up against. Long-gone are the days of throwing my clothes in the washing machine and coming back when the buzzer goes off. This is probably the thing that I miss the most, besides a shower. It just takes a lot of work to live here, especially on the days I have to haul water for the washing machine from the well down the hill.

Debit cards: Nowhere, and I mean nowhere, takes debit or credit cards. This is a 100% cash economy. So what does that mean when you have to buy a $500 bed? You go to one of the two ATMs in town and pull out cash, which only comes in small denominations, take your wad of cash over to the store, and count out your cash. I never carried cash in the States. Here, the only time my debit card comes out is when I need to go get more cash at the ATM.

Church: I liked my church in the U.S., and I love the churches that we can call "home" when we are back on furlough. There is a beauty to what we know. I love the orchestrated order of worship, the words to songs I recognize, the in-depth teachings I receive from well-educated, inspired men. I like doing book studies, helping with children's church, and attending Sunday School. Church in different countries is—well, different. There have been plenty of churches we have attended that just have bad theology. There are churches that are synchronistic, combining the Christian faith with tribal beliefs. There are churches that last five hours. But there are also good churches. Good theology. But church is just different. The typical church service lasts two-and-a-half to four hours. The order of worship is not necessarily structured. The songs are vastly different, and sermons are preached in two different languages—Spanish and the translated tribal tongue. I long for the comfort of church as I know it. I do supplement at home with some good devotionals, Bible studies, and downloaded sermons (on a good internet day) from people I know and trust. But there's just something about a home church. We are plugging into a local church that we trust. The theology is sound. We are involved in worship and attend prayer nights and Bible studies. It's good. It's just different.

Comfort food: A good In-N-Out burger can fill that spot in your belly as any Californian understands. As will a trip to Outback Steak House for that juicy steak, stuffed potato, salad spilling off your plate, and cheesecake for dessert (if there is room). The sushi restaurant down the road or Mimi's Café for breakfast alone with a good book can last me two hours.

Mail: There is one post office in the city, but even after waiting months for our "test" letter from the States to arrive, it still has not come. I don't think we will be sending much of anything through the mail system here.

Do I write these things to make you feel guilty? Absolutely not. Do I write them to make you feel sorry for the poor little missionaries in a third world country? Not even close. So why do I write them? I write them to give you a glimpse of what an average day in our life looks like. I also write it to help you realize the blessings that you have. Even with my "semi-automatic" washing machine, I am ever so grateful that I'm not down at the river scrubbing my clothing on rocks, up to my knees in the water so I can clean clothes for my family. I'm so grateful that I'm not like others in Equatorial Guinea, where the river is unsafe and not nearby, who must use a bucket and a scrub board to wash their clothes. I know that I will have to do that soon as the electricity can go out for weeks here, and I will look longingly at my "semi-automatic" washing machine and hope the electricity will return. Understand, if just a little, about the challenges that others face, and perhaps when you are standing in line at the grocery store, and it is taking a little bit longer than normal, you can reflect on the amazing assortment of groceries you have in your basket, and realize that it's okay to wait a few minutes longer. Or when you are at the doctor's office, and they are running late you can be thankful that at least you have a doctor to go to, a hospital that is safe, medication that is reliable, and diagnostic tests at your disposal. So you can be thankful for your child who has survived past five years old, whereas the average Guinean here has lost at least one child before that age and where a pregnant mother is terrified when it is time to deliver her child as the mortality rate for mothers is so high.

The World Health Organization (WHO) regularly gets together with leaders from around the world to discuss global health issues. They are the impetus behind the efforts to eradicate smallpox, for example. Some of their goals are to establish health-related targets within the Sustainable Development Goals (SDGs), which are then adopted by the United Nations General Assembly. This not only helps evaluate the health of a nation, but helps develop achievable methods of combating some major social injustices and serious health issues around the world.

Here are a few sobering facts the WHO put out in 2015:
Life Expectancy at birth (years)
U.S. - 79.3
Honduras - 74.6
Equatorial Guinea - 58.2 (12th lowest in the world)
Globally - 71.4

Maternal Mortality Rate (per 100,000)
U.S. - 14
Honduras - 129
Equatorial Guinea - 342
Globally - 216

Children less than 5 years old - mortality rate (per 1,000)
U.S. - 6.5
Honduras - 20.4
Equatorial Guinea 94.1
Globally - 42.5

Neonatal Mortality Rate (per 1,000 live births)
U.S. - 3.6
Honduras - 11.0
Equatorial Guinea - 33.1 (15th highest in the world)
Globally - 19.2

Having a global worldview is imperative for a Christian. We are all God's children, and we are all called to be a part of His work in the world. God's calling in the Great Commission is not a request, it is a mandate. *GO!* He says. This doesn't mean the physical act of going for everyone. Sometimes it means praying ardently for missionaries around the world. It means being a part of a missionary's life through financial contribution or encouragement. It means hosting missionaries when they are on furlough, taking them out for dinner, sending birthday cards and anniversary cards. It means fixing their car, hosting their website, and other means of being involved in the life of a missionary. It also can mean going. Going short-term, going long-term. But be involved! Use the items that I listed as prayer points for missionaries and for the world.

Chapter 55

What I Love
About Being a Missionary

I mentioned things that I miss, but there is always a pro for every con. I am a master of figuring things out and using the resources I have. If I can't find it, I figure out how to substitute for it or how to make it. No corned beef for St. Patrick's Day? Let me make my own. I love English muffins—I got that too. Sauerkraut? Yeah, I can make that as well. People used to ask me what I missed, and it got to a point where I stopped missing those things because to continue pining away for things that I will never have is a sincere waste of my emotional energy. So instead, I choose to look at the positive side of these things.

Let's look at those things I miss:

Running water: I've never thought about a well before. I never knew what it was to walk down to get your water, much less drop a bucket on a rope, let it fill, and haul it up. It is a novelty, and as odd as it sounds, an experience I enjoy (for now), and I won't easily forget. I am ever so grateful that I can turn a tap on in the States, and have EPA-approved water come running out and never think twice about it. Getting water from the well for my wash allows me a chance to meet other women at the well who are doing the same thing. It offers a time of fellowship with them and a chance to talk about our kids, what we are cooking for dinner, and what the weather is like—small talk, yet I find comfort in the act of just living and sharing that experience with others. It also gives me a chance to be seen as a Westerner, who is accustomed to the comforts of the U.S., living as they live, doing what they do, and wanting to be a part of their lives.

Flush toilets: We are taught to be good stewards of the earth. Here in Equatorial Guinea, that means conserving water. In Honduras I got used to using a latrine with a hole cut into the ground, and when there was no latrine, finding the closest bush. I have been in countries like Haiti, where a trip to the bathroom was almost more than I could bear. In Sri Lanka, where I had to pee behind a rock, I heard a noise behind me and looked to see a monkey sitting there watching me. I can truly say, "Been there, done that." I am so grateful for the toilet I can sit on and the bucket of water I can use to empty the bowl. I am so grateful that I don't have to use leaves or newspaper as toilet paper. I'm grateful for that toilet that I can't flush.

Dishwasher: The daughter of friends on the mission field made a very interesting and very MK statement. "Mom, I wish that someone would invent a machine that washes dishes." She had never been in a home with a dishwasher. I am the dish washer in our household. I scrape all the food off the plates (as we don't have a garbage disposal), wash the dishes in one basin, rinse in a second basin, rinse again in a bleach-infused water basin, and then set the dishes on the dish rack to air dry. While I wash dishes, I have my music playing in the background, and I enjoy looking out the window at God's creation. We live on a very beautiful property. Outside my window are palm trees, freshly cut grass, ducks that come by to see me for a treat, and a multitude of brilliant birds that can only be found in a rain forest country. Washing dishes doesn't take mind work; it's somewhat cathartic. The simple act gives a feeling of accomplishment while affording me the opportunity of soaking in a peaceful view.

Hot water: In the States, I never looked at electricity as a commodity. It was just always there. I lived in California through the time of rolling blackouts. We were notified of the blackout times far in advance by mail, on the radio, and on the news. So we were prepared for the one-hour or four-hour blackouts. But the complaints were everywhere! I was even grumpy about it. What if I wanted to cook at that exact time? I needed to run my AC extra cool right before the blackout so my house wouldn't get above my comfortable seventy-two degrees. A water heater uses electricity, and it is a luxury that few people in Equatorial Guinea have. Even in hot Honduras and super-hot Africa, taking a cold shower takes your breath away. Remember jumping into a cold lake on a hot summer day as a kid? Now imagine that every time you take a shower. But electricity is a commodity that we value when we have it, and somehow learn to live without it when we don't. We live like nationals and like a large part of the rest of the world.

Shower: I have a hose that sticks out of the bathroom wall that brings in water from the well. More often than not, the well is tapped out and we can't use the shower, so we use a foot-pump camp shower. I step into the shower with my lavendar-scented soap and my loofa, and I step out totally clean. I've not had to go to the well, collect my water, and take a bucket bath. I've not had to go bathe in the river. I have the luxury of taking a shower in privacy. I've taken showers in the rain. The torrential downpours that hit us are amazing. Typically, those type of showers come after dark, and no, I don't strip down, but I do go out in shorts and flip flops, and raise my arms and my face to the heavens, and let the rain pour down on me. I feel carefree like a little kid, and I laugh and giggle while I'm doing it. If Madison is here, she is right out there with me. The simple, carefree act of showering in the rain is joyful, fun, and refreshing.

Car: I've had a car since I was old enough to drive. My mom gifted me the family's 1967 VW Fastback. I learned to drive on a stick, and I visited San Francisco with my friends all the time, so I became an expert at hill driving with a stick. In the Army, I bought a car and traveled all around Europe in that little car. In the U.S. I owned everything from a 3-cylinder Geo Metro to a Ford SUV. In Honduras, we purchased a car four months after we arrived there. In Equatorial Guinea, however, we have decided not to buy one. Here is where I have the choice to be grumpy about that or to live in reliance upon God and the sufficiency He has provided for me. I don't have to buy gas, tune up my car, or be asked for bribes every time I go out. I live like the nationals, and I am not contributing to the pollution in this country. I get lots of walking exercise, and I get a chance to enjoy God's creation every time I go out. By slowing down to a walk, I get to see people living life. Not long ago I walked by a large group of men that were hanging out in front of a house and playing Mancala. They had constructed their own version with wooden boxes and different colored rocks. I felt like I had stumbled upon a very special time for these men. It was their version of a bowling league or chess in the park. It was joyful! I stood there with a goofy smile on my face and just watched for a little while, enjoying witnessing these men in fellowship over an age-old game of Mancala. If I had been driving down the road, I would never have seen this moment, and I would have missed a part of the culture and the friendship that was so evident.

Potable Water: In my time with our mission agency, I've had a few trainings that have involved water safety. In my Disaster Response training we hiked out into the hills and camped alongside a river that had been tested positive for giardia. It was from this water source that we were to get our drinking water. We were taught a method for purification, and we all managed to return giardia-free. In Haiti, at one of the camps we stayed in, an agency was there purifying water. But it was our group's policy that it didn't matter in what manner we received water, we were still going to purify our own. So we took the water we were given and put our own methods to use. In a few days, more than 200 people in the camp were stricken down with diarrheal diseases directly related to the water. Not a single person on our team got sick. So I know what it is to live for a time with non-potable water. God had already prepared me for our time in Africa. In Honduras, we could drink the water from the tap, and we also had a truck that came by multiple times a week for water delivery. The WHO has determined that there are three countries in the world where less than fifty percent of the population has access to potable water. Yes, you guessed it,

Equatorial Guinea is one of those places. The number two cause of death in this country is diarrheal disease. So, we came to Africa prepared, with water filters in tow. I look at my fresh, clean, double-filtered water, and drink without any care. I don't worry about diseases I may get; I don't have to worry about my child getting ill. I drink my water, make sun tea with it, put it in bottles in my refrigerator and drink it cold on hot days. It is a luxury indeed.

TV/Internet: In a country with only two TV stations and where only about twenty percent of the population uses internet, neither is a priority. There are no wasted days sitting idly watching TV as the world passes me by. I sit out on my front porch and listen to the voices of children playing tag and soccer and climbing trees. Adults sit outside and visit, singing together and socializing. It is a wonderful sound to hear. It reminds us of our childhood in the States when we were outside riding our bikes, going to the park, and walking to the store for a Slurpee. Childhood obesity was a rarity. People had hobbies: sewing, painting, reading, playing board games. We have lost so much of that, and I've regained so much of that, being here. I don't have access to a sewing machine, so I'm hand sewing. I've made all sorts of things with the beautiful African fabric I can find at the market. I've learned to crochet, and am reteaching myself the piano on a keyboard I brought with me. My book list is long, and gardening has returned. Without the distractions and the constant input from TV and the internet, the right side of my brain has been reawakened to new things.

Fruit: Yes, there are many, many, many fruits I miss. But one day, when I return to the States, I will be missing the amazing fruit I have had the opportunity to experience here. If you've never eaten a passion fruit, a lychee fresh off the tree, or a water apple, then you've definitely missed out. If you have not had the opportunity to try the slimy and odd, yet surprisingly good, taste of a guanabana, or a papaya you picked off of the tree in your yard, or a pineapple you chopped off of the plant before you brought it in to slice it up, then you've missed an amazing experience. If you haven't had the chance to walk through the endless booths of an African open market and glance at things you have never seen before, buy them, and bring them home to try and experience, then you've missed out on a simple pleasure of life. Yes, there are things I miss, but the many amazing things I've experienced can't be replaced.

Clothing: There's something to be said for simple living. In the States, my huge walk-in closet was filled to capacity. There was clothing that I had never worn because I just had too much. I had more shoes than I would ever use, a dress for every occasion, and season-coordinated shirts and outfits. I had scarves and accessories for my outfits, and I enjoyed shopping. And I truly felt I lived simply. I was not a Macy's shopper or a high-end shopper—I couldn't care less about name brands. My go-to stores were Old Navy and Target. But my closet was full. My dresser was full. Then we moved to the mission field. In Honduras we were still able to wear pretty much whatever we wanted. So I just scaled back. I got rid of my winter clothes, but at least four duffel bags were packed full of my clothing. Then we moved to Africa. The cultural clothing of women here is skirts, and long skirts at that. So away went my pants, my shorts, and my sleeveless shirts. And now my husband and I share a tiny little closet: he has his half and I have mine. And I have room to spare. There's something to say for living simply. I grab a skirt and a shirt, put my sandals on, and I'm ready for the day. There are no matching scarves, no purse that goes with this skirt. There is my one purse for every day. It makes choices easy and allows me to live simply, like the nationals do. Home-sewn clothing, skirts made from fabric purchased at the market, and a head wrap of the same material to go with it. Beautiful.

Convenience: In the States, if I forgot to pick up something I needed at the grocery store, I simply got on the Safeway website, ordered the food, and it was delivered in the next two hours. If I didn't feel like cooking, Boston Market was quick access on my way home from work. Trader Joe's was a personal favorite of ours. Delicious food that was already prepared, or partially prepared, was right down the street from our house. Need something you can't find in town? Order it on Amazon to be delivered overnight. Need a ride to the airport? Uber and Super Shuttle were just an app away. But let's look at all those things. Do we need any single one of those things?

I'm a planner. I max out the planning category in the Myers-Briggs assessment. I like planning for the day, planning for tomorrow, and planning for a year from now. My husband and I have our Google calendar filled in with dates including our next furlough and conferences two and three years from now. You get the picture.

Not having access to any conveniences puts your brain in a different mode. This is where my planning comes into play. I'm utilizing the skills that God has honed in me. I'm also readjusting myself to a simple life. With that comes the understanding that all those things are just things. I value the little things in life once again. I value the joy of simple cooking with basic ingredients. I don't feel the pressure to have everything always just right, because it's impossible. I'm giving myself allowances that I had not given myself before. I'm resting in the sufficiency of God and all that he provides for me. It's an enlightening experience.

Education: So what does an education bring you? In a perfect world, students have access to music, physical education, math, reading, science, history, after-school programs, drama, clubs. This helps a child to be "well-rounded." But what about looking outside of themselves? Where is the education of living life? Where is the education of helping a child on the street by providing food and clothing? These are the educational elements that we were able to provide for our child. Yes, she learned all the normal things (albeit at a lesser quality than in the U.S.), but she learned a second language. She learned about what the rest of the world looks like. She has been to twelve different countries in her twenty years. She knows what it is to live in a third-world country; she knows the blessings that the United States has. She has a worldview that very few young adults her age have. You can't teach that in school. Yes, we "deprived" her of a great private school education, but what we gave her instead are tools and experiences she will use for the rest of her life. That's an education worth having!

Red meat: My body is sorely lacking iron. I am chronically anemic, to an almost dangerous level. I tried to supplement, but my body decided that ferrous sulfate was my nemesis. Before I scratched the top inch of my skin off, I had to stop taking ferrous sulfate. So I try to get iron in what I eat. There are really only two types of green leafy vegetables here: one is a tasteless lettuce, and the other is a very odd, very common, everyday vegetable called endung. But we just can't find a way to cook it that we like. I finally found a consistent source of frozen spinach. So I cook it in lots of our meals and have a mostly spinach omelet a few days a week. In the States and in Honduras, my primary source of iron was red meat. I love it. I grew up in a family of meat eaters. But here it's not an option. So we eat chicken—lots and lots of chicken. The nurse in me rejoices. I've lost ten pounds since we've been here, and that's without trying. I am sure my arteries thank me, my cholesterol thanks me, and my gut thanks me. Being forced to eat healthy also makes me feel better. Don't get me wrong—the first time I hit the States, one of the first restaurants I visit will be the local steak house. But I must embrace the forced healthy living, and honestly, I do.

Radio/movies: I keep talking about a simple life, because I think we've forgotten what that looks like. In our rush to be the perfect family, raising the perfect child, providing opportunities and experiences, we don't know what it is to just sit and be. When I was at home, I either had news on the TV or talk shows on the radio. As soon as I got in the car, the radio came on, and I was listening to music or catching up on the news. I was constantly bombarded with information, input, noise. When I moved to Africa, I realized that this was not going to be an option. With the internet what it is, we can't stream much of anything. And with no radio, I'm only interrupted by the sounds of the birds chirping outside, the ducks coming to my door for a snack, the children playing, and life happening around me. I do read the news once a day to keep up with what is going on in the world, but it's no longer a constant in my life. I find that I am less burdened with maintaining a constant vigil on what is going on. It's quiet.

Health: It is difficult to find an upside to this. As a master's-prepared public health nurse, I am extra-focused on the social injustices of the poor healthcare in most third-world countries. There are some worse than others, and Equatorial Guinea is one of the worst around. Unfortunately, because of the lack of healthcare, people turn to traditional medicine. In many countries, this is an accepted form of practice, using precise, tried-and-true herbal remedies. Here, however, that means something very different. Witchcraft is the primary source of traditional healing. People with life-threatening diseases turn to the witch doctor for healing, and oftentimes die of the treatments themselves. Where I can find the positive in this is in my ability to provide good medicine to those who seek me out. I am grateful to be able to hold medical clinics and give appropriate medicine with appropriate dosing for each illness. It allows me an opportunity to pray with people and to teach them about the Great Physician. So although I see people all around me suffering from illness or succumbing to contagious diseases that they should have been vaccinated against, I can find the Hope that is in Him who sent me to serve His people.

Washing machine: A physical task with a clear goal and a feeling of accomplishment can't be overlooked. Washing clothes has been the job of almost every woman in the world since the dawn of creation. I've had times in my life where I've gone to the laundromat to wash clothes because we couldn't afford a washing machine. I spent three weeks in Haiti washing my clothes under the hose while I was wearing them. When we first moved to Honduras, I hand washed our clothing in a sink and hung them on hangers in the bathroom to dry. But for most of my life, I've had a washing machine. Before we left for the mission field, I saved up to buy a Bosch front-loading washing machine and dryer. They were a dream. They were huge, efficient, and they left my clothes smelling fresher than ever. But, as with washing dishes, there is something cathartic about washing clothes. Your mind can wander over the happenings of the day, and you finish feeling satisfied and accomplished once this simple task is done. I am outside, so I can enjoy the feel of sun on my face and the wind in my hair. I see other women in houses around me hanging their clothes on their own lines. We are living life together. I am grateful for my semi-automatic washing machine that makes my task a little easier than other women who are bent over their buckets to wash. I rejoice in my simple washing machine, and honestly, I don't long for my $1600 washing machine back in the States.

Debit card: Stolen credit card numbers, illegal purchases of over $3000 on your debit card, a stolen wallet. These are things that have happened to me, and I'm sure have happened to many others. There is a simplicity in handing over cash to receive something. There is fun in haggling over prices and in trying to find the best booth with the freshest tomatoes, and then handing over your money for your prize tomatoes. Money has been around for a very long time. The act of putting to paper the value of something and purchasing an item in exchange for that paper money is something that is lost in the States. I never carry cash in the U.S., and here I only carry paper money. But it is like returning to a simpler time of life. I enjoy the feel and the look of the currency here, and no one will be stealing my credit card information any time soon!

Church: Have you ever been in a conga line to give your offering? It is not only a joy to see, but a joy to be a part of. I've never before seen such joyful giving! God asks us to be joyful givers:

"Give generously to him and do so without a grudging heart; then because of this the Lord your God will bless you in all your work and in everything you put your hand to." - Deuteronomy 15:10

Proverbs 21:26 – "The righteous gives and does not hold back."

"Then the people rejoiced because they had offered so willingly, for they made their offering to the Lord with a whole heart, and King David also rejoiced greatly." - 1 Chronicles 29:9

"Now this I say, he who sows sparingly will also reap sparingly, and he who sows bountifully will also reap bountifully. Each one must do just as he has purposed in his heart, not grudgingly or under compulsion, for God loves a cheerful giver. And God is able to make all grace abound to you, so that always having all sufficiency in everything, you may have an abundance for every good deed." - 2 Corinthians 9:6-8

"In everything I showed you that by working hard in this manner you must help the weak and remember the words of the Lord Jesus, that He Himself said, 'It is more blessed to give than to receive.'" - Acts 20:35

The first time we went to a church where the congregation started dancing during the offering, I didn't know what to do. But then I found myself caught up in the conga line, swinging my hips, waving my arms, and dancing to the music as I worked my way up to the offering bucket. It was amazing! I truly did feel joyful and cheerful as I gave my offering to God. Church here is nothing like church in the States. Africans are unafraid to raise their arms and dance in the pews while they raise their voices and sing praises to the Almighty. You can't help but join in. The delight they have in worshipping God is contagious! I think it's something we could learn from this amazing culture. It's not what I am used to, and I do miss what I know. But to see another culture, folks singing in a different tongue to the same one God, gives me goosebumps.

Comfort food: There is not a single fast-food restaurant in the entire country. In Honduras, I was able to fulfill a few vices: we had a Subway, Quiznos, KFC, Burger King, Popeye's, Chili's, TGI Friday, Pizza Hut, Little Ceasars, Wendy's, and even a Denny's. Then we moved to Equatorial Guinea. The closest quick food we have is a place called "Express." They serve traditional Guinean food and can serve it up in about two minutes. But it is local food, not what we know as "comfort food." So you figure out new comfort foods. In Honduras, that meant baleadas. This is a staple food made of a fat tortilla with refried red beans, cheese, and an assortment of other things added to it. It also meant pupusas. This delicious quick bite is a tortilla filled with cheese and fried. How can that not be delicious? So we came to enjoy new comfort foods. When we would arrive back in Honduras after a long trip away, as we were waiting in the airport for our transportation, we wouldn't hit the Wendy's in the airport like most other expatriots; we would head over to the "tipico" restaurant in the food court and get ourselves a baleada. So we find the things in our life that may be different than what we are used to, but they become the new "norm." And there is definite comfort in that.

Mail: No junk mail, no political mail, no bills, no flyers from the local grocery store. There are definitely a lot of benefits to the lack of mail where we are. The downside is obvious—if we can't find what we want here, there is no ordering it. There were no sympathy cards when my father passed away, no correspondence from our churches. But the beauty of modern technology is we are only an e-mail away. Keeping up with us is as easy as a click on your computer, and an "I'm thinking about you" e-mail can fill my tank for a while. So although not having mail is a bummer, it is simply a convenience issue, but that's about it. So while you are thinking about it, send an e-mail to someone who you haven't been in touch with in some time. Give a missionary an e-card, a "I'm thinking about you" note. Reach out to an MK on the field and tell them you prayed for them. Mail comes in new forms in this day and age, but don't forget to take advantage of it.

Chapter 56

Now it's Your Turn

There are a lot of books written about short-term missions teams, their impact on the communities they serve, and the people who go on them. Some of my favorites are *Go and Make Disciples* by Roger Greenway, *Let the Nations be Glad* by John Piper, and *On Being a Missionary* by Thomas Hale.

That being said, I would love to share some personal thoughts about working in a short-term capacity. Romans 10:14-15 are by far my favorite missions verses: "How, then, can they call on the one they have not believed in? And how can they believe in the one of whom they have not heard? And how can they hear without someone preaching to them? And how can anyone preach unless they are sent? As it is written: 'How beautiful are the feet of those who bring good news!'"

How do I pray for teams coming? I pray that their lives would be changed. That they would be ever outward looking. That they would impact lives. That they would love on people. That they would be blessed by those they have come to serve. That they would be stretched. But I also pray that things don't always go well. I pray for some discomfort—heat, lost bags, broken-down cars, supplies not arriving, cold   showers, discomfort because you have to throw your toilet paper in the trash rather than the toilet, food they dislike, eating only PB&Js for a week, working late, not working at all, not drinking the water, sleeping ten to a room. You get the idea. I truly pray for these things. Why?!

It's so easy to become accustomed to the creature comfort in life. Most of us are so self-centered (and I include myself in that statement). And yet we go on a trip for just a week or two and complain a whole lot! We enter into the lives of people that live this life every day. We live it for a week. How many of us could have lived in the wilderness and eaten locusts for dinner? How many could have been like Jesus who went into the desert on faith alone, knowing He would be cared for? How many of us truly and honestly have a motivation to reach out to others from our heart, and not a desire to feel good about it? To be loving and caring when we aren't being observed? To show kindness and mercy without having pictures taken of us?

So, my question to you, my reader, if you have been or will go on a short-term trip is, what is your motivation for going? In the book *On Being a Missionary*, Hale makes the statement: "Being a missionary begins with being called. You don't choose to be a missionary; you're called to be one. The only choice is whether to obey."

There are so many people who, in their heart, believe they are called to missions. They come to the field, but end up leaving the field disheartened, discouraged, and not having accomplished much of anything. I call this a "heart call." In your heart you feel led, and yet, God has not necessarily called you to this purpose. Does that mean being a missionary that has been truly called is a missionary that makes things happen? Plant ten churches, see a hundred people saved, build a school. No, it means being obedient to the One who sent you—having an open heart to go where God calls. To repent when we stray from His path. To pray for opportunities that you may not want. The bottom line is to be obedient.

When you go on a short-term trip, realize that twenty-five gringos in a village of 3,000 Hondurans is quite a spectacle. But I pray that you look at how you present yourself. Are you putting on a show, or showing your love to others? Are you feeling good about what you are doing, or feeling the hearts and hardships of those you have come to serve? Are you staring in awe about how "the poor people live" in their dirty, rotting home, or rejoicing in their eternal home? Search your heart for your motivation. Go with an open heart. Go being prepared to serve. Go without an agenda. Go and be love—the love that comes by serving our great and awesome God. Imitate Jesus who loved the poor more than the rich, Jesus who showed mercy and kindness without bringing a single dollar, Jesus who loved the little children. Be that kind of missionary. See how God will stretch you, love you, break you, and use you.

We hear we need to "pay it forward." Don't get me wrong, I think this is an amazing idea. I love it! However, we need to consider our motives. Years ago, long before we ever went on the mission field, I helped a young man who had tipped his wheelchair over and couldn't get up. I stopped my car and got out to help him. I set him back upright and sent him on his way. But my pastor asked me, "Why did you stop and help him? Were you thinking about what others thought about what you were doing, or were you doing it because it was the right thing to do?"

My earliest memory is as a four-year-old saving a baby bird that had fallen from its nest. I begged my preschool teachers to save this poor little creature. As an adult I realize that this was hopeless, but as a young child of four, my world was wrapped around this little bird.

God put into me a need, a mandate to help others—people, animals, it doesn't matter. My husband has been so frustrated with me at times. One day I made him pull over so that I could relocate a praying mantis that was on our windshield to the forest floor before we drove on. I rescued a robin that flew into my windshield and took it to the vet. I picked up a tarantula that made its way into our house and escorted it back outside to do its job. I've given food to the starving and clothed the naked. I can't pass by the needy. It's a bit overwhelming at times. I feel overcome, but the God-script in my soul tells me to help those who can't help themselves.

He has told you, O man, what is good; and what does the Lord require of you but to do justice, and to love kindness, and to walk humbly with your God? - Micah 6:8

Then I look at my motive. What is my motive? Do I do it without others seeing? Yes, I've administered CPR to a bicyclist hit by a car, attended to a man who flew through a windshield because he was not wearing a seat belt, delivered a baby in the earthquake-torn country of Haiti, and comforted a man who lost his whole family after a tsunami swept them all away. I do it because I am called to do it. I do it because I can't not do it. My heart hurts when others hurt.

Search your heart. Do good to others, not because society is watching, not because you want to be seen. Do it because you won't get the accolades. Do it because you won't be seen by others, because God sees your heart and He knows why you do it.

"...The LORD does not look at the things people look at. People look at the outward appearance, but the LORD looks at the heart." – 1 Samuel 16:7

Chapter 57

The End?

I come to the end of this book—to the end of these adventures and I don't even know where to stop. There are so many stories to tell, and so many more yet to come. And yet, I know that I must conclude somewhere.

How do you finish a book about God being in your life? Honestly, you don't. Because that journey isn't finished until you have run the race and finished what He has set out for you to do. I love the words from the Westminster Catechism that remind me of my purpose as I set out to accomplish what He has placed before me each day. What is the chief end of man? The age-old question—*Why am I here? What is my purpose? Why was I born into this place, this time?* The answer is clear and succinct: "To glorify God and enjoy Him forever." Forever. When I have finished this race and stand before Him, I will enjoy Him for eternity.

In the words I learned during my training to be an Evangelism Explosion instructor: *Why should I let you into my Heaven?* God asks.

I pray my answer is simple. Because I love You and your Son, and I know that I am only here because You chose me. You chose me from a family of beautiful, loving parents, but those that weren't believers. You chose me apart from who I was.

Romans says it perfectly: "but God shows his love for us in that while we were still sinners, Christ died for us." – Romans 5:8.

And my life verse: "For by grace you have been saved through faith. And this is not your own doing; it is the gift of God, not a result of works, so that no one may boast." – Ephesians 2:8-9.

And the verse I have tattooed on my ankle: "So now faith, hope, and love abide, these three; but the greatest of these is love." - 1 Corinthians 13:13

These are verses that have helped guide me through this journey called life.

- God has led me on this grand adventure. He has more adventures to take me on, more heartaches, more circumstances that I will feel completely unequipped for, and yet He will equip me. He is sufficient. That is the theme that resonates throughout this book. That God is sufficient. He is sufficient for me, for my circumstances, for others. He sustains me throughout and equips me to be able to move on to the next circumstance.
- We will see where this grand quest of life leads me. I'm sure there is going to be another book just about Africa. Because without question, He will lead me down paths I don't wish to go on and will show me things I don't want to see. He will help me be there when someone dies and when someone is brought into this world. I realize how very small I am, and how insignificant. And yet in that, God has seen fit to use me for His glory. With the words of the woman who came to our clinic, and the words that will remind me of why I am here, "I come here because Jesus is here." And the words I long to hear at the end of my race,"Well done, my good and faithful servant."

Punto. The end. 'nuff said.

For more information contact:

Erin Pettengill
C/O Advantage Books
P.O. Box 160847
Altamonte Springs, FL 32716

info@advbooks.com

To purchase additional copies of this book visit our bookstore website
at: ww.advbookstore.com

Longwood, Florida, USA
"we bring dreams to life"™
www.advbookstore.com